# Praise for Allies & Angels

*"Allies & Angels is about parenting and faith and living authentic lives. It explores the ways in which we can support our children through love, kindness, compassion and acceptance. It highlights what can happen when we have the love and support of family and others who are open-minded enough to become part of a life changing journey. As a professional advocate for the trans\* and gender non-conforming community I reap rewards beyond any expectation. The Cook's are a significant part of those rewards. They have found a way to share this story, acknowledge all that contributed in some positive way, critique those who wish us harm and highlight significant challenges others face when they don't have support. Read this book if you want to know how to parent your children through any challenge, big or small, significant or fleeting. Come to understand that "suppressing and rejecting" a [transgender] child robs them and adds tremendously to the already existing burdens that are part of life. This book is a gift that teaches that a change in perspective can have a miraculous impact in ways unimaginable."*
—Sheilah R. Sable, Director of Organizing for the Empire State Pride Agenda

*"Allies & Angels is a story that has the power to open your heart and your mind. Terri and Vince show us what it means to wholly and unconditionally love our children as the wonderful people they were meant to be. Their story is one of compassion, learning, and support that anyone who has or works with children and youth can understand and relate to, even if they don't know someone who is transgender. Their family's journey, through both laughter and tears, offers hope to families and young people going through similar experiences. After reading Allies & Angels you will certainly walk away with a greater understanding of what it is like to be transgender. If you allow yourself to, you will also understand the joys of loving someone who is transgender."*
—Marissa Rice, Director of Youth Services, AIDS Community Resources

*"Once I started reading Allies & Angels, I didn't want to put the book down. Reading this took me back 20 years when I came out to my parents. I wish there had been a book like this for them. This book reminded me of struggles others face when we come out as transgender. As someone who works with transgender youth, Allies and Angels provides an important perspective on the lives of transgender youth through the eyes of two parents. By sharing their struggles with coming to terms with Drew's transition and then dealing with the world around them, Terri and Vince offer hope to transgender people, their family and friends ... and help others understand what it means to be*

*transgender. This book is a must-read for not only parents of transgender children, but anyone who knows someone who is transgender."*

—Rob Pusch, Syracuse University, Associate Director at Project Advance and Q Center transgender youth group facilitator

*"Allies & Angels has an urgent message, but it does not tell you what to think—instead it shows, through the powerful, heart-wrenching narrative of a loving family, what a difference individuals can make in the lives of transgender youth. I hope it becomes the go-to book for the parents of such kids, and that it inspires the same kind of compassion and respect shown by Drew's family. It should be required reading for all who work with children and young adults of any gender. I'm a little older than Drew, but also grew up in the suburbs of Syracuse, New York and also came out as transgender in my teens. I faced many of the same issues, from big things like bullying and suicidal depression to so-called little things like the pain of school dances and old family photos. Although few struggles compare to being a young man in a female body, there still is little guidance available for these boys or their loved ones. I wish such a book had existed for me and my parents during those difficult years and I hope this helps such families realize they aren't alone. It will definitely improve, and most likely save, many young people's lives."*

—Elliott DeLine, Author of *Refuse* and *I Know Very Well How I Got My Name*

*"Allies & Angels is a powerful story that would benefit anyone interested in growing in love and understanding. It certainly benefited me. The story provides you with a comprehensive understanding of not only what their son went through, but the entire family, when discovering their daughter is really their son. It's a book that anyone should be able to relate to as a parent, a friend, as a human being. It will hopefully open the eyes of those who are quick to judge, and to instead "walk in somebody else's shoes." The Cooks could be your best friends, your neighbors, relatives or classmates. They give an honest and inspiring account about the power of love, courage and acceptance."*

—Tami Scott, Editor of *Allies & Angels* and *Baldwinsville Messenger*

*"As someone who came out only six months ago at the age of 22, and whose parents are in the early stages of understanding and acceptance, this book was very emotional for me. The Cook family's story is so inspiring and heartfelt. Thank you for making yourself vulnerable and writing this story so that others may find hope and come to better understand the experiences of trans\* people and their families. I can only imagine what my life would be like now had I had the strength, courage, and support that*

*Drew had, in particular from his family and the Q Center, to come out at a younger age. A great book for anyone to read—whether you're trans\*, you have family or friends that are, or you just want to learn a little bit more."*

—Al Forbes, Syracuse University graduate student

*"Live authentically." "Find your passion." "We are all connected." These are familiar concepts to those of us in the self-help, life coach, and spirituality realm. I've read a lot about these ideas, but it's a whole other experience to watch the Cook family live them every day. Now with their new book, Allies & Angels, others can benefit from their enduring story of love and acceptance. This book is a real life example of how living authentically, finding your passion, and realizing that we are all connected can bring more love, joy and compassion into your life. The knowledge and understanding gained by reading this book will make you an angel in someone else's life. In my mind, there is no greater gift that you could give yourself and the human experience."*

—Gloria Ierardi, Life Coach

*"I remember when I first talked to you. I hung onto every word of your emails... literally... they were my only hope. I never felt so alone and so scared for my son and prayed for myself to gain some understanding. As you know... families should not have to go through crisis to that extent. A book like this would have been priceless to me. You and Vince will be helping so many people with this book. Thank you for being there for me, Terri. You don't realize it, but you and the Q Center gave me understanding where I had very little. I am a much better person for it. Just take a look at my son... he is happy. That says it all."*

—Laurie, Nurse and parent of a transgender son

# ALLIES & ANGELS

*A memoir of our family's transition*

Terri and Vince Cook

HALLOWED BIRCH
PUBLISHING

# Allies & Angels
## A memoir of our family's transition

### Notice

Mention of specific companies, organizations, or authorities in this book does not imply endorsement by the authors or publisher, nor does the mention of specific companies, organizations, or authorities imply that they endorse this book, its authors, or the publisher.

Internet addresses were accurate at the time of writing.

*How to Live* lyrics © 2012 Billy Cook used with permission.

Books from Hallowed Birch Publishing may be purchased for business, promotional use, or special sales. Contact Hallowed Birch Publishing at hallowedbirchpublishing.com.

Tami Scott, Editor

Library of Congress Control Number: 2013912040
Printed on acid-free paper.

ISBN: 978-0-9894027-0-5 Paperback
ISBN: 978-0-9894027-1-2 Hardcover
ISBN: 978-0-9894027-2-9 eBook

hallowedbirchpublishing.com
Marcellus, NY

*To Billy…*
*for teaching us how to live.*

*To Drew…*
*for helping us see who we are*
*and who we want to be.*

*We love you both so much, more than words can say.*

# Contents

# Contents

# Acknowledgments

There is no question that the Q Center through Aids Community Resources had a part in saving our son's life. We gratefully acknowledge the following people for their generous support of the Q Center.

M. Daniel Bingham and M. Gail Hamner

Michael Crinnin

Sally J. Gould and Victoria H. King

Cathy Leogrande

Kevin and Ludger Viefhues-Bailey


*Allies & Angels* is all about the people who helped us on our journey. The following people are allies having provided generous support to ensure our story gets published and heard.

Mark Pultorak

The Ierardi Family

The Sgambati-Stevens Family

Sandra Lee Fenske and Joe Silberlicht

Sheilah Sable and Sesame Campbell

Angela Vernieri

Tami and Tim Scott

Tabitha Bachofer

Jean Lovett

Bill and Patti Ossola

Mike and Sarah Curtis

John Jastrebski

Writing this book was possible because of countless allies and angels in our lives. We've written about many of them in the pages that follow, but there are several more that we wish to extend our deepest gratitude and thanks to:

Our families, in particular, our parents, sisters, brothers, aunts, uncles and cousins. We've been so blessed that you have shown us unconditional love, support, and acceptance on this long and difficult journey. Thank you for your support and encouragement of our mid-life career shift as we passionately dove into writing this book and dedicating our lives to a higher purpose.

Tami Scott, our talented, supportive, and insightful editor. It was divine intervention that brought you into our lives! You helped structure and polish our story into a book that makes us proud. You are a gifted and talented writer and editor. More importantly, you are a kind, compassionate, human being who we know will remain a good friend for the rest of our lives.

Gloria Ierardi and Rachel Smorol, the kind of friends every person should be blessed with. Gloria, you are a truly gifted life coach. We were so fortunate to have you coach and guide us throughout your Martha Beck Life Coach Training. Thank you for not only introducing us to Martha's inspiring brilliance, but for helping us create a life that is truly authentic and joyful. Rachel, you've been by our side for nearly thirty years, loving and supporting our children every day of their lives. We're so grateful for our weekly get-togethers and the never-ending support, encouragement, and friendship you both have provided.

Our Q Center family, especially Heather Crate, Tyler Sliker, Michael Crinnin, Maureen Harrington-O'Neill, Marissa Rice, Carrie Portzline-Large, Rob Pusch, Mallory Livingston, Karen Fuller, Teri Coon, and all of our friends in the TransParent group. Thank you also to all the Q Center youth and young adults who have inspired us to raise our voices.

Rhys Harper, for all of your contributions … from photography, to video, to web design, to promotional materials, and of course, for your friendship, encouragement and support of this project.

Our "secret friends" from Thursday nights, especially Max, Keyhan, Kathy, Craig, Jackie, Scott, Gail, Joyce, and many others. You gave us the skills, support, strength, and hope we needed to change ourselves, get out of the way of our children, and live life one day at a time. Thanks for helping us learn that despite challenges and unsolved problems we can do more than get by, we can thrive!

Our Lockheed Martin family, especially Sandy Fenske, Ray Hajzus, Charlie Moore, Pat Purtell, Mary Lanzafame, Kathy Tedford, Cheryl Costa, and the PRIDE leadership and members. Each of you helped us more than you'll ever know. Thank you for your support and friendship during the most challenging of times.

Sheilah Sable, from Empire State Pride Agenda, for your encouragement, support and review of our book … and for the many opportunities you provided to speak, train, advocate, and refine our views as allies. Your dedication continues to fuel our passion.

Betty DeGeneres, for the inspiration you don't even know you provided when you spoke at the Lockheed Martin LGBT Leadership Forum in 2012 and then when you signed your book (*Love, Ellen*) for Terri. Your passion and advocacy, unconditional love, and your wonderful book, have been an inspiration for our own life path.

Jack Canfield, for the success principles and life skills you've inspired and developed in both of us since the late 1980s. Over the years you've helped us achieve many successes, but our breakthrough goal—to write and publish a book which can help change and save lives—for this we are most grateful. We thank you for sharing your advice, experience and lessons learned about writing, publishing, and marketing a book. We also thank you for your Success Principles Coaching program. Our exceptional coach, Gary Reid, guided us through the life changes we needed to achieve this breakthrough goal. Thank you for using your life to help others achieve their greatest vision. Thanks to you and Gary, we've overcome the fears, obstacles and limiting beliefs that nearly kept us from completing this book!

The following people who read the manuscript and provided us with valuable feedback: Al Forbes, Tyler Sliker, Elliott DeLine, Sheilah Sable, Gloria Ierardi, Marissa Rice, Rob Pusch, and Rachel Smorol. Thank you for taking time out of your busy schedules to provide your comments.

And finally, although this book is dedicated to both of them, we also wish to close with acknowledging our wonderful children, Billy and Drew. The two of you have brought so much joy and love into our lives. You have made us better people. We thank you for encouraging and supporting us as we wrote this book and for all the sacrifices you have made so that we could pursue our passion and purpose.

# Foreword

My name is Drew. I'm the son you are going to read oh-so-much about in this book. My parents have always dreamed about changing the world—helping people—and I never doubted them once. This book is just one of several steps toward reaching that dream. They have already helped so many. I am extremely lucky to have parents like mine.

Like any teenager, I like to think everything is about me, but my family's lives were affected by my transition almost as much as mine. Experiences like mine are rarely talked about and resources for what my parents went through are practically nonexistent.

I hope that I can help others by enthusiastically supporting my mom and dad as they bravely put their faces, lives and feelings up for public scrutiny. Although I fully support my parents in this endeavor, I'm not going on the book tour or doing any interviews to help publicize their book. I got a late start being Andrew, and I'm ready to begin a new chapter in my life—just as my parents are starting a new chapter in their lives. I look forward to meeting new people in college, and I don't want to be known as "that trans guy." I want to be known for my character and achievements, not for my medical condition. I am finally getting to be a teenager and have a plain old normal life. I hope you can understand, respect, and accept that.

This book is for those who are in my situation, or my family's, or for those who just want to open their mind to a life experience that differs from their own.

Thanks for reading our story. I hope you like it. I hope it changes you and makes you a bit more aware of the struggles that so many people like me have gone through and continue to go through. I hope it makes you more of an ally, not just to trans people but to all people.

—Andrew "Drew" Cook

# Chapter 1

# Introduction

*The greatest obstacle to discovery is not ignorance—it is the illusion of knowledge.*
*—Daniel Boorstin*

**W**hen you first find out you're having a baby, you often think about all the beautiful moments and memories you have ahead of you. You read books to help you learn about parenting, to prepare you for any circumstance that may come your way; even if those techniques get tossed out the window as soon as your baby cries or delivers his first tantrum!

You think of all the fun ways you'll teach your child about nature, about life, about love and compassion ... Truth is, at this point, you rarely if at all think about what the child will teach you.

Children are constant reminders of all things new. When a child first sees a flower bloom, first hears a kitten's purr, or feels the first blunt sting of a bumble bee—it becomes a first time for you all over again. And this time, you see things differently. Children become the teachers, we become the students, and our world forever transforms us.

My husband and I wrote this book to share a difficult life experience—something we learned from our child, which indeed forever transformed us. Our hope is that by being vulnerable, by taking this chance and telling our story, others will find our experience useful, comforting, and enlightening. We follow in the lead of many that have gone before us and shared their stories. Their courage has been our blessing.

As proud parents of two young men, we faced something that wasn't covered in any of the parenting books we read. You see, we didn't always know we had two sons. Our younger child was born a girl and for fifteen years we believed we were raising a daughter. Our precious child, who we now know is our son, is transgender.

It has been, and continues to be, quite a journey for our family. We supported our teenage son with his transition from female to male.

If you happen to be, know, or love somebody who is transgender, this memoir may warm your heart. If this subject is foreign to you, if it's a topic you know very little about, your initial reaction may be one of discomfort or judgment.

Many people who haven't had much exposure or education about being transgender typically experience a range of reactions, from shock, fear, and curiosity, to anger or disgust. Common responses are:

*How could a child know who they are or what they want at that age?*

*What kind of parent would let their child do something like that?*

*I don't care what age the person is, that's wrong, or it's a sin.*

*How could you allow your child to make irreversible changes to their body with hormones and surgery?*

*As a parent you have to set rules and boundaries for your children, protect them, and not allow them to make choices that will affect the rest of their lives.*

*You have failed as a parent by allowing your child to make choices that a child isn't old enough or mature enough to make.*

I understand these feelings, questions, and statements. I certainly felt shock and fear. I, too, asked several of those questions—and many, many more. I had to get answers—and unlearn the myths, lies, and stereotypes previously assumed—because my son's life depended on it.

Gender identity, your internal sense of being male or female, is usually taken for granted. For most of us, our gender identity matches the body we were born in. It can be very difficult for people to understand what it means to be transgender, or to understand any experience that is different from their own.

I've come to understand that most people *think* they know what it means to be transgender, but more often than not, their understanding is flawed. Many fail to understand that gender identity is permanently developed in the brain and not directly related to your sex organs. Being transgender is not a choice or a decision—it is a medical condition that nobody would choose to have.

Imagine being born with a medical condition that you could not control and you did nothing to cause. Imagine that because this medical condition causes so much pain and suffering, almost half of the people with this condition attempt suicide. Imagine that rather than receiving empathy, support, and compassion for your medical condition, you received rejection, harassment, discrimination, and acts of violence against you. To top it off, imagine that there were no laws to protect you from this injustice.

My son's struggle to understand, accept, and *simply be who he is* nearly cost him his life. Forty-one percent of transgender people attempt suicide. My son is part of that shocking statistic. He has come a long way since those days, but it has not been easy, and the challenges are not over for him, or for us.

In this story, we hope you will relate to us and recognize that we're an intelligent, loving family, trying to do our best. We're the neighbors next door, your childhood pals, your work colleagues or former fellow classmates—we might hang out, reminisce, laugh together, and be friends.

My husband and I have been married for twenty-four years. We're smart, hardworking, caring people who love each other and our family very much. When we were younger, we put ourselves through school and earned our master's degrees. We worked hard in our professions, climbing the corporate ladder, and doing our best to support our families. We've both served in public office in various capacities because we believe in serving and supporting our schools and community. We both volunteer and contribute generously of our time and money.

When we weren't busy working or cheering on our two kids at the various events and activities they participated in, we'd hang out with family, friends or neighbors laughing over a beer, a glass of wine, or cup of coffee. When our children were little, I was blessed with the opportunity and made the choice to put my career on hold so that I could stay home with them. Our kids also benefitted and thrived in daycares when it was needed.

We did all the things we thought responsible parents were supposed to do to raise healthy, happy, successful children. We made many choices and sacrifices, which we believed were the right thing to do at the time. We sought help and guidance along the way because we knew we weren't born with all the answers. We are ordinary, occasionally boring, occasionally hilarious, average people.

I wish we could tell our story in a way that first introduced you to our family and our amazing son, Drew, without you knowing he is transgender. If our story could play out from the beginning, I'm certain you would feel the pain, the heartbreak, and the struggles along with us. You too would experience the unthinkable and go on a desperate search for answers while trying to save and support somebody you love with your whole being. You would learn what we learned, and face the choices and decisions that we faced. Maybe, you would make the same choices.

For some people, their religious or moral understanding trumps all arguments, love, and compassion to the contrary. They feel compelled to exercise judgment that no one can challenge. So we won't.

For everyone else, we hope you can read our story with an open mind.

### We Can Be a Bridge

One of the reasons we are telling our story is because we can help people understand in another way. We can be a bridge. You may not relate to or understand the transgender issue, but you can possibly relate to us as people and as parents. And by connecting with us, you might come to understand something you may have never been exposed to nor had a need to learn about.

Vince and I took our gender identity for granted. Our gender identity matches the bodies we were born in, and we found it difficult to understand how our son could be different. If you asked me several years ago what it means to be transgender, I would have provided an uneducated, and possibly insensitive, response. We "fit" neatly in the boxes that society, for the most part, finds acceptable and even desirable. We were blissfully ignorant of other people's experiences because we conformed to what most people around us expected.

## Invitation to Our Journey

One of the best teachers is experience. I know that when someone tries to convince me of something, I back away. It actually turns me off. In fact, I may already agree with you about something, but the act of you trying to convince me turns me off so much that I may begin to question and doubt my previous belief!

However, if I have an experience, then my mindset can be changed instantly.

Not everybody will be blessed with knowing or loving a transgender person, so not everybody will have the gift of our experience—the gift that changed our mindset.

Vince and I are sharing our family's experience. We do not intend to preach, tell you what to believe, or "convert" anybody. That would send me running in the opposite direction, and no doubt it could do the same for others. In telling our story, we're simply inviting you along as we discovered and further explored our beliefs. This experience has changed us, and we're inviting you to experience our journey.

## Because We Had to Learn

We have gained so many incredible gifts as a result of life events that we never would have chosen for our family. There was little time for self-pity and questioning why. We had to jump in, open our hearts and minds, and learn what we needed to learn. We weren't able to control or change the situation. Being transgender is not a choice for our son; it's an inherent part of who he is, and has been since the day he was born.

Since I learned what it means to be transgender, I now look at all people differently. I now look at others the way I hope they would look at me or my child. I'm able to look for goodness in others and find the many things we share in common. From that place, I'm able to open my heart and decide what I can do differently to support and validate or affirm, rather than judge.

Learning my daughter is really my son ironically taught me who *I am* and who I want to be. My son's transition was medical and social. My transition was somewhat social, but mostly spiritual. This has undoubtedly been a spiritual growth experience for me. I now see what connects all of us. I feel a oneness and a shared experience with all of humanity.

Every one of us matters. And every one of us has the power to make a difference, befriend and support one another, and change the world.

All my life I lived as a popular, accepted, and successful person. I was secure with myself; confident. Yet, when I learned I had a transgender child, my world as I had always known it turned upside down. I became frightened; fearful that if I told the truth—that my son is transgender—people would judge or criticize me or my son. I experienced what it feels like to be different; to not fit in, not be accepted or understood. Whether my fears were real or perceived, it didn't matter. Fear, in and of itself, is paralyzing.

Not knowing who is and isn't safe to confide in is part of the quandary. You can't look at somebody and know whether that person is an ally, somebody you can confide in without judgment. If it's a friend, you don't always know if they will remain your friend, or gossip behind your back and quietly drop out of your life. I came to understand what the term "safe space" means. I came to realize how many things I took for granted, because I lived a "privileged" life.

I'm not proud of the fact that I experienced fear and insecurity. Why should I care what other people think? What do I have to be afraid of? I'm not a teenager struggling to get through adolescence, yearning to fit in and be accepted by my peers. I am an adult now; a successful, well established one at that.

But I do need to care. I need to care for my son's safety and well-being. Violence, harassment, discrimination and rejection of transgender people are dangerously real. Needless disclosure would expose my son and could inadvertently put him in harm's way. The statistics of murder, violence, and hate crimes against the trans community are horrifying. Sixty-one percent are victims of physical assault. Sixty-four percent are victims of sexual assault. Compared to the general public, trans people in the USA are approximately ten times more likely to be murdered. People who are transgender are twenty-eight percent more likely to experience physical violence than those who are gender normative.

I need to be honest about my feelings. I cannot and will not paint a picture of myself as the "perfect parent"—a fictitious, model of virtue. I was scared and insecure, and it was hard. Let me be perfectly clear, my son has always had my unconditional love and support. However, if it were possible, I might have chosen to hide from the world rather than let people know my child is transgender and deal with their potential rejection and judgment, or worse.

For me to grow through this and model the behavior I would want my children to see and embrace for themselves, it was crucial for me to confront my feelings. In order to better understand why others are uncomfortable around gender or sexual identities that differ from their own, it was vital for me to understand why I was uncomfortable, and learn how to bring about the change in myself.

Since my eyes have been opened to all that I don't know about the world and the people around me, life has become magical. The more I can accept and embrace all that I have learned, the more I can make it safe for others around me to do the same.

The story to follow may shock, sadden, anger, or challenge you. It may do all of those things. My greatest hope is that our story will also change you and inspire you to be an ally.

**Chapter 2**

## Our First Son is Born

*God, grant me the serenity to accept the things I cannot
change, the courage to change the things I can, and the
wisdom to know the difference.*
—*Reinhold Niebuhr, The Serenity Prayer*

**W**e had done all the right things during her pregnancy. Terri took
her vitamins. We stayed active by walking everywhere. We read all
the books. We had our paint roller to massage her back in labor,
which they taught us about in Lamaze. We went to every doctor's
appointment together. We did our breathing the way it's supposed
to be done. A nurse was now advising me.

*As with all surgeries, there is the risk of infection.*

*There may be additional blood loss and hemorrhaging.*

*She will need to stay in the hospital an additional four days
to recover.*

*She can have a reaction to the anesthesia.*

*She may require additional surgeries if there are complications.*

*There is the risk of death.*

Terri had been taken from the very comfortable, home-like birthing room where we had spent the last four days. She was being prepped for a caesarean section while a nurse went over the surgery risks with me.

How did we find ourselves in this situation, didn't we do everything perfectly? Too strong for tears to flow freely, my eyes instead felt like they would pop out of my head. My rational mind had long since retired after four days and nights with my wife in labor. The words "risk of death" rattled me. We had only been married two years. I wanted to sob uncontrollably, but I couldn't.

Terri had a difficult labor with Billy because she wouldn't dilate. I remember thinking Terri's contractions were registering strong enough on the monitor, but they still put her on Pitocin. The doctors and nurses were watching the baby for signs of distress, and we were content to keep trying.

We were committed to a drug-free labor, meaning no pain killers, but the Pitocin made Terri's contractions so intense that perhaps surgery became a welcome relief to Terri. Not for me; I was terrified.

Terri and I were at one end of the operating room table, a green curtain between us and the doctors. She had had a spinal and was wide awake. Yes, she was wide awake after four days of labor. I sat nearby while she just laid there. We were ridiculously in love and gazing at each other, trying to be brave. At last, we heard a wet "plop" as Billy came out. The doctor said, "His head was really wedged in there." I peered around the curtain expecting to see what he meant. It was just gross.

We joke that because Billy's head was stuck at a funny angle and wouldn't come out, Billy was in there thinking, *wait, I know the way. I know what I'm doing.* We joke because that would become a typical situation for Billy as a child. He would always be so sure he knew what he was doing and so adamant in doing it his way, despite the reality or consequences.

But everything about baby Billy fueled our love for each other. Everybody was fine. The doctor informed us that Billy had an extra thumb. It didn't matter—that would easily be corrected with surgery when he was a little older. We were happy new parents.

My new role as Dad kicked in quickly. Soon after he was born, my job was to gently rub his chest under the warming light. My son and I were alone together for the very first time. I cried another manly cry—with no tears. I loved him instantly, from the moment he was conceived. Now, we were just meeting in person.

Looking back now on Billy's extra thumb, I can't help but wonder if God was easing us into what was to come with Drew. We had to accept that our son was born with an extra thumb and live with it until he was old enough to have it surgically removed. We had to explain the extra thumb to friends, family, and curious onlookers in public places. And we had to make decisions under the advisement of medical professionals regarding when or even if the extra thumb should be surgically removed, considering what Billy's life would be like if we chose not to have the surgery. Certainly Billy could wait until he was eighteen and decide for himself whether to keep or remove the extra thumb. However, what would his childhood be like living with the extra digit? What kind of teasing and bullying would he endure during his youth? What activities would he not be able to participate in due to this birth defect? Sure, his grandmother could knit custom winter gloves for him, but could we buy a baseball mitt to fit? Doctors told us the extra thumb was drawing energy from his primary thumb and if it was not removed by the time he was two years old, then his primary thumb would never grow as large as it should. If we made Billy wait until he was old enough to decide for himself whether to have surgery, he would have physical limitations that we could have prevented. Looking back, Billy's extra thumb provided many parallels to what was to come with Drew. We don't regret our decision to have Billy's extra thumb removed, and we don't regret any of our decisions to support Drew's medical transition. Interestingly, nobody judged us or questioned our decision to allow Billy's surgery.

We hadn't planned to have children so early in our marriage. We were both in graduate school, but Billy was a miracle. This may sound suspicious, but I swear Terri and I both heard a spiritual message telling us that it was the right time. I don't know who said what, but I remember that we both knew Billy should be conceived that night. Some people wait and wonder if they are really pregnant. We knew immediately when our baby was conceived.

We prepared to be the best parents ever to "Billy-Jo," the affectionate name we used from the contraction of the boy and girl names we had selected from the beginning of Terri's pregnancy.

Somewhere we learned that an unborn baby would bond to the sound of our voices. So, we both sang to him a lot before he was born. Billy-Jo seemed to love musicals, too. We bought season tickets to Music Theater North and felt him kick and dance to the rhythms all season long inside Terri. After he was born, singing to him was the magic ticket; it quieted him down instantly. But there was one catch: we couldn't stop. We ended up recording one full side of a cassette singing the same few children's songs over and over. Our acapella mix-tape saved us on many a five-hour car ride to grandma's house.

As a child, Billy was extremely unselfish and cooperative. In order to make playtime more fun, he often gave his stuff to other kids who were more difficult or demanding. He was very polite and endearing. He was also shy, but popular and well-liked. He was gentle.

Billy was reading, and learning Spanish and sign language at his daycare prior to kindergarten. When we found out his daycare offered kindergarten, we enrolled him and he really took off. Unfortunately, the daycare only offered kindergarten. The other local private school options required a lengthy drive for a six-year-old. So, Billy entered public school for first grade.

The public school did not have a gifted program, was crowded, and was generally ill-equipped to provide adequate stimulation for Billy. It was a constant struggle for us and the teachers to keep Billy engaged, challenged, and motivated. He was a straight A student throughout elementary school, and earned honors status in middle school until his grades started to drop because he refused to do homework.

If a difficult labor was Billy's entrance into the world as a boy, a difficult adolescence was Billy's transition into the world as a man. Fours days of intense labor; four years of severe adolescence struggle. Again, it would be expensive and involve many doctors, but this time it was much more painful for all of us.

In eighth grade, Billy's circle of friends changed dramatically. Innocent at first, he would later succumb to drugs and delinquent behavior by high school.

Billy stopped participating in school, refusing to do classwork and homework. He had gone from being an honors student to failing his classes. In tenth grade, he failed five out of seven courses, despite having A's on his final exams. Billy even scored top ten in the state on a national French assessment, yet failed the course with a twenty average. He was required to attend two classes in summer school, where he received A's in both classes. Schoolwork was extremely easy for him, but he failed to see the point in doing it.

He began to abuse drugs in the summer before tenth grade.

We soon realized Billy's drug use had gone beyond gateway drugs, and he was in serious danger of addictions that are extremely difficult to overcome. Our personal experience and judgment told us that the drugs he was taking could have lasting negative consequences if we didn't intervene. Billy's rejection of rules and authority was also a major concern and needed to be addressed before the drug issue could be resolved.

We hired an educational consulting firm to help us, and we fully supported their recommendation that Billy attend an intensive wilderness program, followed by a longer-term residential program where he could finish high school. This recommendation came after a thorough evaluation of Billy's academic, psychological, medical, and legal history, as well as in-depth interviews with us and numerous professionals, to get to know Billy's unique needs. There are lots of great programs out there, but even the best program in the world isn't necessarily right for every person. We wanted to find the perfect fit for Billy's specific needs because at the time, we really believed we had only one shot at interrupting his self-destructive cycle and saving him. To do so, we made the decision to spend his college fund.

The programs that Billy attended were necessary but not enough to heal our family. The power struggles of adolescence were mostly gone; but, our family still teetered on the brink of disaster. Terri and I needed a program, too; a recovery program. We found Families Anonymous (FA), a 12-step program for parents like us. Through FA, we learned to give Billy the keys to his life and get out of his way. Once in the driver's seat, Billy made better choices.

All too often a parent's conviction to keeping their child safe will manifest all sorts of desperate behavior leading to obsessive attempts to control their child. We were no exception, and without a program ourselves, we would have sabotaged Billy's recovery and succumbed to our bad behaviors.

We are so proud of Billy for not giving up on himself or our family. We survived each other.

We don't want to share much more about this period of Billy's life, which is thankfully now behind us. We were reluctant to mention it at all because it is only a snapshot of a period of time and in no way representative of who he is. As you read about the years to follow, you'll hear of the loving big brother who proudly embraced and supported his little brother and bravely stood up to intolerant peers. That is more indicative of who Billy is—loving, loyal, courageous, strong—and we couldn't be more proud of him.

We mention this time in Billy's life for two reasons. The saying, "What doesn't kill you makes you stronger," is very true in our case. Our family is much stronger and closer than it might have been had we not had this experience. The second reason is that I don't know that we would or could have handled Drew's situation with the compassion and delicacy he needed. Throughout our story you'll hear references back to how our experience parenting Billy prepared us for what was to come with Drew.

Our experience with Billy taught us to dig deep—to keep a critical eye on our assumptions, to reach out, to get therapy for ourselves, and to keep an open mind. We learned to embrace the Serenity Prayer, which helped us let go of things we couldn't control and save our minds and our energy for better uses. As much as I know Billy wishes he could go back and change those years, we recognize that those years helped save all of our lives.

Paraphrasing what one of Billy's therapists once told us, "What we need to learn and the changes we need to make as parents, to help the situation, is just good living." We took what Billy's therapist said to heart as good students of life and we did find his words of wisdom to be true. We found a good life through the changes we made in ourselves. Our trials with Billy helped us learn *how to live.*

One evening during his second year of college, Billy came downstairs and made us listen to a new song he had recorded. Terri was openly crying when she heard it. I had another manly cry. We had our Billy back. His lyrics have since become an inspiration to us, and they are an anthem to Drew's struggle, as well. We've included his song, appropriately named, *How to Live*, at the end of the book.

---

### An Ally Pays It Forward

Not long after the trouble began with Billy, we let on to our friend, Jim, the nature of our family problems. To our surprise, our friend shared his similar experience, which in turn, dramatically changed the course of ours. It was comforting to hear about his struggle. His story let us know we were not alone.

Looking back, he might have been "paying it forward." That is, despite the pain his family experienced, someone may have helped him along the way by sharing an experience. Our friend left us with this advice that has served us well: "You can get through this crisis. It may take a long time. It will take a lot of patience and commitment. Your family will not be the same, but it can be better."

For us, it did get better. Five years later, our son is in control of his life, and we are all living one day at a time. All is not perfect; we still have our personality warts that make us human, but we are no longer controlled by day-to-day power struggles, rebellion, and chemical dependency.

We are grateful for our friend's advice and that fateful day we dared to share our secret. He is an example of a true ally. In the most humble way, he offered us hope. He has no idea how much he helped Terri and me get through many a sleepless night or the confidence he gave us to press on when we thought it was hopeless.

Jim demonstrated a deeper understanding of the issues and the compassion of someone who has been there.

In contrast, there will always be people willing to spout off ignorance, which we've learned to mostly ignore. Here is an actual example of such ignorance, written in a local letter to the editor:

### To keep kids off drugs, parents must shape up

*To the Editor:*

*Regarding the letter March 12, "End of the failed Drug War" – if parents did their jobs right, children wouldn't grow up to use drugs, et al. Then there wouldn't be a "Drug War."*

*Since it seems obvious that some parents have failed to do their jobs right, maybe the police should arrest those parents and charge them with child endangerment when their children are arrested. Get the picture?*

*Let's face it: We mold all the children. Let's break the mold and be better parents. Talk with your kids, and listen to them with an open heart.*

*By the way, I never had any children, I wish I had. I'd like to think I would have done right by them.*

Judgment of parenting from someone who isn't even a parent is difficult to swallow. Although many readers may not be able to relate to parenting a transgender child, there are countless many with a child or loved one who has drug, alcohol or behavioral problems. Although there are exceptions to every generalization, I venture to guess most readers know that good, responsible parents can find themselves with a troubled child. Judging *all* parents—declaring they should be arrested—comes from ignorance.

The ignorance and judgment we faced as parents of a child using drugs is nothing compared to what we continue to face as the parents of a transgender child.

The letter writer got something right though. "*Talk with your kids. Listen to them with an open heart.*" Those words couldn't be truer ... for all parents. If you listen, truly listen, with an open heart, you may not hear what you want to hear, but you'll hear what you need to hear.

# Chapter 3

## Drew's Beginning

*There is nothing in a caterpillar that tells you it's going to be a butterfly.*
—*Buckminster Fuller*

**V**ince and I were sitting together in my doctor's office waiting anxiously for the results of a blood test. Our fears were heightened: the test indicated a chance of Down syndrome. My doctor suggested doing amniocentesis to know for sure and wanted us to proceed right away.

We didn't know the risk to our baby until the nurse informed us that the procedure does pose potential risks. The risk of miscarriage is one in two-hundred. She might as well have stopped there.

We asked why we would have a procedure that would pose such a risk to our baby and why we were being rushed to decide. The answer was "…because you are in the $n^{th}$ week. There is still time to terminate the pregnancy."

The thought shook us. Not an option. Not for us. We had been trying for months to get pregnant. Together we agreed that we didn't love and want our child only if he fit a certain criteria.

We were having our baby and we would bring him into a loving home where he was wanted no matter what.

Then the nurse left us to discuss and sign the consent. Well, that did not happen. There was nothing we were going to find out that was worth risking our son's life. Period.

A few weeks later we settled for a high resolution ultrasound—a procedure which posed no risk to our baby but would give us more insight into his development, allowing us to prepare if he had special needs. The ultrasound showed his heart developing quite normally and all tell-tale anatomical measurements looked good. Ironically, in researching this event we found Drew's ultrasound printout buried in a box of analog pictures we planned to do something with someday. The doctor had written "Think girl" on the picture and drew an arrow pointing to the area between his legs.

Like Billy-Jo, Drew's name before birth was a contraction of the two names we had selected, Joe-Jo. The doctor's note changed nothing because we wanted to wait until birth to be sure of our baby's gender. Sure ... right? It was almost fifteen years until we knew for sure.

Throughout the book I will use male pronouns, even when describing my son Drew as a child. When I speak of the fourteen years before learning he was transgender, before he transitioned—even though at the time he was living and presenting as a girl—I'll still be using male pronouns.

We are at a place now where Drew is and has always been a boy—our son. Even when I look at pictures, where he was clearly dressed as and looked like a girl, I now see my son. Even in pink, with ribbons and bows in his hair (which were always my choosing, not his) I see my little boy. I so clearly know now that he has always been a boy.

We have made the decision to be true to who he is throughout the book, and we hope that the reader can read from this perspective. We want to expand the strict, binary (or boy-girl) perspective of gender.

## Drew had a Happy Start

When Drew was little, he was healthy, happy, and full of life. Well, that's not entirely true. Billy was an angel from the beginning and the reason we wanted to have more kids. Drew was the reason we stopped. Until Drew could talk, he was quite irritable, especially in the evenings and when he was tired. But he was a very smart baby, too. We look back at that time and theorize that his inability to communicate his thoughts must have really frustrated him, and therefore rolled over into his behavior.

After Drew learned to talk, however, he was every bit as wonderful as Billy with his own special brand of wonderful.

Drew was never a fan of dresses or dolls or stereotypical "girl things." Instead, he climbed trees wearing T-shirts and jeans.

"Mommy, this is too scratchy!" or "Mommy, I can't jump and run when I wear that!" Often he'd pretend not to see the cute little dress or outfit I had laid out for him. His favorite clothes were his big brother's hand-me-downs.

After he got dressed each morning, he'd throw his arms around me, squeeze real tight, and plant a big kiss on my cheek.

"Let's go play, Mommy!"

And then he was off running with the kind of energy, joy, and excitement that causes most adults to pause, smile, and wish they were young again.

When Drew turned three years old, I took a break from my career so that I could be home while the kids were little. This was my second attempt at being a stay-at-home mom. Before Drew was born, I tried to come home for Billy. However, mom was no match for the fantastic day care Billy attended. He soon wanted to go back with his friends. As with all things Billy and Drew, where Billy hated it, Drew loved it.

In 1998, I watched a lot of Oprah and kept a gratitude journal. Our children were ages seven and three. We had been married all of nine years.

We were living our lives as happy middle class Americans. During that time I began writing a book, intended for my kids, which I never finished. The book reads like a gratitude journal that chronicles the simple everyday joys of our experiences as a young family. In it I wrote:

> *I think my children are very fortunate. They are grow-*
> *ing up in a home with both parents, who are still very much*
> *in love with each other. Their dad has a very successful*
> *career. He spends far more time at home with our family*
> *than he does at the office. Vince's job pays very well and*

*has outstanding benefits, so (although we are not wealthy by any stretch of the imagination) we live very comfortably and have all that we need, as well as the means to help our parents through their retirement. Their mom has chosen the role of "stay-at-home mom," so I am available to get the kids off to school in the morning, greet them when they return home from school, stay home with them when they're sick, and volunteer full-time at their schools. We have family dinners together and (usually) have enough clean laundry and (usually) have the house in a decent enough state that unexpected guests are a welcome surprise and not a frightening prospect. In the eyes of some, you might say we are living the life of a modernized 50's-sitcom family.*

*I say that we're "modernized," because I don't equate myself with the role of the 50's-sitcom housewife. I have an advanced college degree and had a successful, high-paying career in the corporate world. I have lived on both sides … the working mom trying to balance a career and family, and the stay-at-home mom who occasionally yearns for the value and recognition that I received at the office. (The life of a stay-at-home mom is much more challenging, yet garners very little respect… and certainly no financial compensation!)*

*Despite the challenges, frustrations, and lack of financial rewards that go along with being a stay-at-home mom, I must admit that I am happy … in fact, sometimes deliriously happy!*

Oh, the irony and bittersweet memories looking back and reading the blissful words I had written fifteen years earlier.

I think the best way to describe Vince and me back then is "parents with attitude." We were doing it right. People told us so. We thought we were doing all the things necessary to raise happy, healthy, successful children who would never do drugs, never get into trouble, and never need therapy. We secretly, unconsciously (and sometimes consciously) judged others who didn't do it right. Our kids were perfect. Everybody loved them.

Before Drew started kindergarten, I volunteered at Billy's elementary school. Drew would come along with me, helping in the classroom, working the school book fair, and playing at recess while I provided an extra set of hands and eyes on the playground. By the time Drew was ready for kindergarten, he was an old-timer. Everyone knew him.

Drew loved school and couldn't get enough of it! He wanted to do it all and got involved in almost every club and activity offered: Student Council, Running Club, dance, Science Fair, Art Club, Chess and Checkers Club, Girl Scouts, softball, basketball, intramurals, and the school musicals. He had many friends, but there was a small group of girls that he became friends with in kindergarten who remained close. As the girls grew older, they did everything together and I became very good friends with their moms.

Drew was the silly, playful one in the group. You know, the one we say, "marches to the beat of a different drummer." When the girls would dress up like princesses, Drew would dress up like a puppy, or he would put on a silly, brightly-colored, mismatched outfit—backwards. Being "girly" was never his thing, but he had wonderful friends who loved him and let him be his silly, playful self. When his interests or preferences differed from the other girls, it was never an issue; it was "just Drew."

In fourth grade, the moms of his close girlfriends asked me what it was that we were doing as parents to raise a young girl with such high self-esteem that she didn't get caught up in all the "girl drama." Drew didn't care about wearing makeup, getting pierced ears, buying clothes, or trying to fit in with the popular girls. He appeared oblivious to all of that, while the other girls were slowly becoming obsessed and changing before their parents' eyes.

Of course, we thought the same thing about Drew and his high self-esteem. We were proud of him and perhaps a little too proud of ourselves. It never occurred to us that he wasn't caught up in girl drama because he wasn't actually a girl. Why would it? We figured Drew was a late-bloomer and were grateful for the extra time he got to be a kid.

Although I was glad that he could care less about girl drama, I did wish he would at least comb his hair, or let me put it up in a ponytail. His long hair was always a disheveled mess and each morning and night was a horrible ordeal, filled with tears and dread, as we combed out his hair and tried to untangle it. Drew hated having his hair brushed and it broke my heart whenever it came time to try. I swear I tried every detangler and conditioner on the market, but was never able to make it an easy or pleasant experience. The best it ever got was bearable. We figured he had a sensitive scalp and considered ourselves lucky and blessed if this was our greatest trauma. When the tangle torture was over, Drew would look up at me, sometimes with tears still in his eyes, and smile to let me know it was OK and that he loved me.

If there were one quality I wish I could convey about Drew growing up it would be his loving, forgiving, and compassionate spirit. Despite having his hair tugged and yanked by me, he wanted to make sure I knew that he still loved me and he knew it wasn't my fault. He had every right to get mad and blame me, and while most kids might argue or rebel, Drew did not. He was worried how I was feeling, despite the tears in his own eyes and the sting on his own scalp.

### Nesting Hugs and Dance Parties

Drew was known for his quick smile, his giggle, and his hugs. At home especially, he'd comfort us with what he called his "nesting hugs." It was a magical sort of hug, where he'd wrap his arms around the top of your head and hold you close but very gently. It was like a mother bird wrapping her wings around her chicks to keep them warm and safe without smothering them. We don't know where he learned this beautiful hugging technique, but I know that my husband and I tried to master it throughout the rest of his childhood so that we could return the gift. There's nothing more I could want to do as a parent than give my children the same feeling of love, safety, and acceptance that we felt when wrapped in one of Drew's nesting hugs.

Another fun memory I have of Drew growing up involves our Saturday night dance parties. We'd push all the living room furniture against the walls to create a big dance floor in the center of the room. A local radio station played disco and dance music from the 50's through the 80's. Drew and I would spin and dance and laugh at ourselves until we collapsed on the floor. I would teach him the Twist, the Locomotion, the Hustle, and the Bump when those songs were played. He would teach me the crazy dance moves he made up in between.

Sometimes we'd dress up in hats or wear something silly from his dress-up box. Thank goodness for the living room curtains because we really did "dance like no one is watching!" Our Saturday night dance parties are a wonderful representation of what my parenting experience, before adolescence, was like—happy, joyful, silly, musical, and full of laughter and smiles.

There is also an indomitable spirit within Drew. On one trip to Disney World, he proudly exclaimed, "I'm not afraid of anything!" everywhere we went. On another occasion, Billy and I were standing and screaming on Billy's bed while Drew and Vince dug through Billy's closet looking for a mouse. When the mouse ran down the hall, they chased it together.

Vince and I always said we wished we were more like Drew, and it was because of his kindness, his spirit, and the way he made you feel when you were around him.

Now that you know how happy, loving, and outgoing Drew was as a child, and have a sense of what our parent-child relationship was like, I hope you can grasp how significant and devastating the changes that followed were. The erosion of his smile and dimming of his bright spirit were much more than typical adolescence, even though many people tried to convince us that's all it was. It was heartbreaking to experience.

## Chapter 4

# Winter Break Eighth Grade

*Do not pray for an easy life, pray for the strength to endure a difficult one.*
*—Bruce Lee*

It was approaching nine o'clock at night and I realized Drew had been up in his room for several hours. My husband and I were worried about the increasing amount of time he isolated in his bedroom. We made it a point to check on him regularly. We tried to connect with him. We tried to get him to spend time with the rest of the family or his friends.

I left the kitchen to make my way upstairs, turned the corner, looked up, and froze in my tracks. There at the top of the stairs was my beautiful child standing, shaking, slowly rocking back and forth with tears streaming down his face—and covered in blood. His eyes were glazed over; he looked as if he was about to tip over.

I can't describe the terror that came over me when I saw him, the panic that filled my body and just paralyzed me. Then primal instinct just as quickly took control of my body and propelled me up the stairs to grab hold of him and pull him to the floor. It was then that I caught a glimpse of the blood on the sheets of his bed.

A portion of that evening remains a blur in my mind. My husband wasn't home at the time. I remember a flurry of activity … grabbing towels or clothing or something to control the flow of blood, figuring out where the blood was coming from, calming him down, calming myself down, assessing the situation, and assuring him that it was going to be OK even though I had no idea if it would. I don't remember getting to the hospital or how I got hold of my husband to let him know what happened and where we were. The next thing I remember is sitting beside Drew as he lay on the hospital bed. His wrists were wrapped in bandages and dozens of scars ran up and down his arms; he turned his head away from me, he couldn't look me in the eye.

Drew had given up all hope and didn't believe his life could ever get better. He wanted to end his life and end the pain. For weeks, months, or longer leading up to this desperate night, he had been cutting himself. He was mutilating his body to feel something other than the pain he was feeling inside. My son was hurting so badly, and although I knew something was wrong, I really had no idea how much until that night.

It was that night at the hospital when I first learned my son had been cutting himself. It was only a few weeks earlier that I even learned what cutting was. As a member of the school board, staff would tell me about issues that our high school students were facing. This particular time, they mentioned cutting and I remember asking what they meant. I went home and researched this term because it was disturbing to me. I was so disconnected from this concept and could not understand, relate to, or identify with it.

Little did I know it was happening under my own roof and that this wouldn't be the last or greatest test of my ability to understand and accept something I had never before identified with or experienced.

## How Did It Get So Bad?

Where Billy had acted out in self-destruction, our therapist told us Drew was acting inwardly. Just as we had believed in our seemingly open, mature conversations about school, drugs, and the law with Billy; we believed in our open, mature conversations with Drew about his life. We thought of ourselves as conservative parents. The phrase, "Trust but verify," was our nature. Both Billy and Drew fell into the life traps that we thought we were responsibly discussing at the dinner table and avoiding altogether *because* of these talks.

Where Billy found drugs to ease his adolescent suffering, Drew kept the pressures bottled up until it became a crisis. The inner conflict causing him such pain was more easily concealed than Billy's more commonly understood form of acting out.

Drew's childhood photos could now reflect a storyboard similar to those used in developing films. Those pictures of a child full of love, life, and promise would be followed by a progression of photos during adolescence when he started to withdraw, when his body was in the picture and he would still look at the camera, but he wasn't present. When his eyes started to lose their sparkle, his enthusiasm for life started to dwindle, and his struggle was just beginning. Then, there came the years of pictures when he would hide from the camera and refuse to have his picture taken altogether. The few pictures that did capture his face showed an immense sadness and pain—a struggle to exist. The light had completely gone out in his eyes.

Those pictures would tell a story that I couldn't hope to match with my words, but for now, my words will have to do. For now, his story can't be told through photos in a way or place that protects him and the life that he's worked so hard to rebuild for himself.

Drew was in sixth grade when we started to see the change in him. The depression, anxiety, and social isolation had begun. The laughter stopped and the smiles began to fade. He went from being a social butterfly and straight-A student to not wanting to leave the house and not wanting to go to school.

This grade would be the turning point in Drew's life. It was the pivotal year we now look back on and say that's where life changed for Drew. Well before he was conscious of it, he could not be himself in a female body much longer.

Drew's teachers had been generally exceptional throughout school, until this particular year. He experienced a lot of conflict with his new instructor, who had a wide reputation for being tougher on boys than girls. We found the tension between Drew and his teacher odd, because at the time and by all accounts, we all knew Drew as a girl.

At the end of the school year, this teacher did not recommend Drew for an advanced math track in seventh grade. This was particularly disturbing because Drew's grades in math dropped from well above average to average that year largely due to these inexplicable conflicts. He loved math and had dreams of becoming a math teacher.

We looked into a private school and enrolled Drew for a summer class prior to seventh grade. We hoped it would rekindle his spirit, and it did. He bonded well with his new teacher, who told us how much he admired Drew, and excelled creatively. It was during this summer course at the private school that Drew became a "Mac" person and convinced us to buy him a MacBook.

Drew had expressed a great interest in attending the private school for seventh grade, but we were hesitant about making the switch, so we waited a full year. This caused somewhat of a setback. Drew lost interest in school academically and bonded tightly with a friend at the public middle school. We can't help but feel we missed the opportunity to switch when the time was right. He transferred to the private school in eighth grade.

Overall, it was a great school. We loved it, but Drew was not happy. When he'd come home, he would prefer to hang out alone in his room and keep to himself. He was feeling the pressure. The new school was academically and socially challenging, he had to wear a uniform he didn't like, and perhaps the toughest part was that he didn't want to let us down because it was expensive and it was he who had originally wanted the change.

If you read the list of warning signs that your child is using drugs, his behavior would fit the criteria: withdrawn, declining grades, and loss of interest in previous activities. Given his brother's history, we were a little worried and sought help. We concluded he was not using drugs, yet we also knew something was very wrong. It could not be brushed off as typical adolescent behavior. We just didn't know what it was. As his depression and anxiety increased, so did our worry and feelings of hopelessness. Watching someone you love in pain and not being able to help him is more excruciating than any pain I've ever experienced personally.

On one occasion, Drew was able to communicate how terribly unhappy he was in a clever demonstration. He threw down a piece of paper with his name written on it. He then proceeded to throw down additional pieces of paper on top of the one with his name. On these papers he had written all the issues and concerns that were burdening him, until he had quite a pile stacked up. It was at this point when we realized that the private school was not going to work. Despite the sunk money, we decided to honor his wish to return to the public middle school.

His first week back started right after Christmas vacation. Drew came home elated that his friends missed him. He was warmly greeted in school and seemed to garner some celebrity status, too. We didn't think much of it after that. We were happy and thought we had made a good decision. The next month seemed uneventful to us, but we learned much later that the honeymoon was short. A few kids discovered Drew to be a satisfying and easy target for their bullying throughout sixth and seventh grade, and they quickly picked up where they left off when Drew returned in eighth. They were merciless.

They taunted him, grilled his appearance—was he a girl or a boy? They knocked him down in the hallways, and laughed at him. Drew kept his torment to himself. It was years later when we learned of the awful things that were said and done to him in the middle school hallways.

It was during winter break, a month and a half after he returned to the public middle school, when Drew tried to take his life and I found him at the top of the stairs.

Drew would be homebound the rest of the school year. The school district provided a tutor that would come to our house for two hours each day. To the credit of the school, the tutor, and Drew, the school year was not lost. Drew finished with nice grades.

Still, problems remained. We did not know about the excessive bullying at school, and we certainly didn't know there was any issue with gender identity. We only knew that Drew was depressed and felt he couldn't succeed at school. He couldn't concentrate and anxiety would lead to panic attacks.

We and his therapist concentrated on Drew's inability to focus in class and the resulting social anxiety as an Attention Deficit Disorder (ADD) symptom. Consequently, Drew tried various ADD medications. The results were probably typical. The first had bad side effects and another didn't work, so we settled on one that seemed to be the most effective. However, Drew still suffered from side effects such as extreme weight loss and migraines. His doctor then prescribed another powerful medication for the headaches. At times Drew was taking two or three medications for depression and anxiety, one for ADD, and another for the migraines.

He was surrounded by people who loved him and wanted to help him, yet that only seemed to contribute to his depression because he and the doctors didn't know what was wrong with him. He believed it when the other kids called him a freak and a loser. He couldn't find the words to describe what he was feeling, or what he was struggling with inside. He knew he was different, but he couldn't tell us—not because he wouldn't be accepted (although later he was afraid of that)—but because he didn't even know or understand the disconnect between his brain and his body.

# Chapter 5

## Middle School Fail

*You must not lose faith in humanity. Humanity is like an ocean; if a few drops of the ocean are dirty, the ocean does not become dirty.*
*—Mahatma Gandhi*

Drew had been on homebound study since winter break in eighth grade following his suicide attempt. A teacher would come to our house two hours each day to tutor him, administer tests, and oversee completion of his schoolwork. On occasion, the tutor would bring fliers home announcing events and activities that might be of interest to Drew, although it was generally assumed that if a student required homebound study, he or she could not or would not be attending extracurricular activities. One announcement was for the eighth grade Moving Up Dance.

Every year, a dance for eighth grade students is held to formally celebrate the end of middle school. Drew paid little attention to this particular flyer. He maintained contact with a few friends from school, so he was well aware of the upcoming affair.

Mike, Drew's best friend, moved away in May near the end of the school year. Since there was less than a month of school remaining, Mike completed the year remotely and was required to come back to school for final exams. With Mike away, Drew had no interest in attending the dance. He didn't want to be anywhere near the other students. His social anxiety was getting worse and being around his classmates was torture. Mike, Ashley, and Kristin were the only friends he cared to see, and he was even beginning to feel like an outsider around them. To attend the dance, even if accompanied by them, would have sent his anxiety through the roof.

The dance was a semi-formal event and the girls were all excited about shopping to pick out their dresses and new shoes. Many of the girls would get their hair done, as well as get manicures and pedicures—all the primping and prepping was comparable to a high school prom. Although the event was semi-formal, not formal, the girls still chose to wear fancy dresses, some very short, some tea-length, and nearly all with spaghetti straps. Nope, Drew wanted nothing to do with that. He hadn't worn a dress in years. It even pained him to have to wear dress pants every day earlier in the year when he was attending private school. He was not comfortable in anything other than his baggy cargo pants, oversized T-shirts and hoodies, and skate sneakers. There was nothing about the Moving Up Dance that appealed to him.

"Yo dude … I'm here!" Mike seemed to yell into the phone. Whenever Drew and Mike spoke on the phone, I could always hear both sides of the conversation. Their voices and laughter would get so loud.

Drew looked puzzled. "What do you mean you're here?"

"Like, I'm right down the street from your house! I had to take the state French exam and I'm here at the middle school. What are you doing?"

"Nothing. Sleeping. Nothing really."

"Dude? Want to chill for a while? Can I come over?"

Drew looked at me and before he could say anything I told him to invite Mike and his mom over. It made me so happy to see the smile start to form on Drew's face. He never smiled anymore. It was as if every day was becoming a chore and he had nothing to look forward to. As hard as we tried to get him out to do things with his friends or with us, he resisted. However, the look on his face at the thought of hanging out with Mike was priceless. He might as well have been on his way to Disney World!

It had been so long since Drew had seen or wanted to see any of his friends. Mike, though, was different. They had been best friends since the day in fifth grade when Mike moved in a few blocks away. They became inseparable, like two peas in a pod, and remained that way until Mike's family moved again. They finished each other's sentences, laughed at each other's jokes, and loved all the same video games, TV shows, and movies. They had the same crazy sense of humor, and seemed like happy little children with a language all their own. They went on each other's family vacations and camping trips. Mike's family loved to have Drew around because it kept Mike happy and busy. We felt the same. Mike became another son to us.

We used to joke all the time that Drew and Mike would probably end up married one day, yet they had no interest in or attraction toward one another. Mike had a girlfriend for a good part of eighth grade. Drew didn't want anything to do with boys and certainly didn't consider Mike a potential boyfriend. Mike was his best friend. We would have been thrilled, however, to see a romance blossom between the two because we adored Mike and because we desperately wanted Drew to engage in some sort of normal teenage social activity, but Drew was clearly not interested. They simply had the best friendship I had ever seen between a girl and boy.

When Mike arrived, they headed for the family room. Their laughter and loud voices filled our home. Seeing them together laughing, joking, and catching up was such a refreshing change from the moping, miserable, withdrawn person who preferred to hide in his room all day. My heart was filled with joy. This was a good day.

Mike's mom and I sat on the deck and chatted for a while. She had errands to run while she was in town so I told her I'd take care of the kids. It seems funny to refer to them as kids playing when they were on the brink of entering high school. Yet, still to this day, when Mike and Drew get together, it is like kids playing.

After a couple of video games, they began to cook up a plan. They wanted to check out the dance. Several of their friends had been texting them and heard Mike was in town. They encouraged them to come to the dance. I don't know how, but Mike convinced Drew that he wanted to go, too. There was safety in numbers, I guess, and Drew must have thought it might not be a bad idea considering he'd have Mike with him.

When Mike showed up at our house he was wearing dress pants and a polo shirt. Shortly after he arrived, however, he borrowed a pair of sweat pants and a T-shirt from Drew. Since they were going to a semi-formal dance, he changed back into his original clothes. Although he wasn't as fancy as the other kids, he cleaned up well.

Drew was now having second thoughts. He didn't want to dress up. "Nah, let's just stay here." Mike wouldn't take no for an answer. He kept trying to persuade Drew to change his mind.

Drew looked at me with a quiet pleading to save him. No such help from me though. I was already going through both our closets trying to figure out something he could wear. I suggested some of my work dresses and skirts. I offered him a simple black skirt that wasn't fancy, frilly, or girly, but he refused.

"I am *not* wearing a dress or a skirt. Why do I have to dress up? Why do I have to go?"

"Come on Drew … it'll be fun," Mike said. "Don't make me go by myself. Come with me, come with me."

At this point it was clear that Mike was going, with or without Drew. He poured on the charm and pleaded some more.

Drew finally agreed to go, but refused to wear a dress. He put on a pair of plain black pants—not dress pants, but neat, clean, black khakis. He paired them with a plain white button down shirt. He completed the outfit with a new pair of black skate sneakers. He didn't own a pair of dress shoes and he refused to wear any of mine, even my simple black flats. Khakis and a button down shirt was as fancy as he would get.

I asked if he would allow me to brush his hair and put it up in a headband or clip. "No," he said in an exasperated tone. "I don't even want to wear what I'm wearing … don't start on my hair. I'll comb it but I'm not putting fancy stuff in it."

That was the best I was going to get—he would comb his hair. That was enough. My Drew was leaving the house and joining his friends at the middle school dance. And as I started to give in about his hair, he seemed to get excited again about going. I was cautiously optimistic. Thank God for Mike and the effect that he had on Drew! From our deck, I watched them walk out of the house and down the street to the middle school. My heart was so happy!

Vince pulled in the driveway shortly after the kids left and joined me on the deck. I had just started telling him how great it was that Mike convinced Drew to go to the dance when out of the corner of my eye, I saw them walking down the street back toward our house.

My heart sank. He didn't do it. I was so afraid of that. He couldn't go through with it; his social anxiety got the worst of him and he couldn't be around the other kids. What a great friend Mike is, I thought, to walk him home, rather than stay at the dance without him.

"What happened?" I was prepared to hear the story of how Drew couldn't go through with going into the school.

"They kicked us out," Mike said.

Vince and I looked at each other, certain we heard wrong.

"Yeah, right. Really, what happened?"

Drew looked devastated and uncomfortable. "I'm getting out of these clothes." And he ran upstairs to change.

Mike sat on the deck with me and Vince. "They kicked us out. The principal said we aren't students there and are not allowed there and he made us leave."

"You're serious? They kicked you out? Did something happen that you're not telling us?"

"The principal wouldn't even let us in. I guess technically he didn't kick us out of the dance, because we never got to go into the dance. He wouldn't let us past the table in the lobby. He said we are not students there and are not allowed in. He made us leave. He yelled at us … and was mad."

I was floored. It didn't make any sense to me. Of course they are students there! Granted, Mike moved away three weeks earlier, but he was completing eighth grade remotely – through *this* school. Hadn't he been at the middle school earlier that *same* day taking a test alongside all of his classmates? And granted, Drew was on homebound study, but he was certainly an eighth grade middle school student who was tutored every day by a teacher from *that* school. Drew was every bit a student; he just happened to be on homebound instruction as recommended by his doctor.

My confusion turned to heartbreak when I saw the look on Drew's face. It took so much for him to muster the courage to attend that dance. He endured the torture of dressing up, and after suffering through the fear and dread and anxiety, a part of him actually seemed excited to go. This was *huge*. This could have been such a big step forward for him in overcoming his social anxiety.

He could have accomplished something he didn't think he could or wanted to do. And maybe he might have had fun and gotten to be a teenager and enjoy something that all other teenagers take for granted.

My heartbreak turned to anger. This can't be so. Why would the principal kick my child out of the dance? He *knows* Drew is a student there. He's a good student, a straight-A student, and not a troublemaker. He has never been in trouble, never been disciplined, why wouldn't he let him into the school? It must be a misunderstanding … the kids must have misunderstood … otherwise, this was completely unacceptable.

I had to go down to the middle school to find out for myself.

I walked to the school and entered the lobby. Two teachers were sitting at the ticket table and several were milling about the lobby, probably chaperones. Among them was the principal. Music spilled into the entryway from the dance and several girls were standing in the doorway between the cafeteria and the lobby.

"Mrs. Cook! Mrs. Cook!" they yelled as they ran over to me, best they could in their high-heeled shoes.

I had known these girls since they were four years old. They grew up with Drew. Several spent most of their elementary school years at our home. We were like family. I had missed them so much; I rarely saw them over the past year. Drew had lost touch with most of them, although I was still close friends with their parents.

They each threw their arms around me and gave me a hug.

"It's great to see you," I said, "You all look so beautiful!"

Indeed they did. Sundresses and fancy hairdos, jewelry and makeup … they looked like princesses! Although I had known these girls for years, I had never seen them look so lovely and so grown up. Drew looked nothing like that when he left for the dance, but then again, that's not Drew. I had never seen him look like that … ever. The last time I got him to wear a fancy dress was for my sister-in-law's wedding six years earlier. He hated it and was so uncomfortable that he never wanted to wear one again. And I never made him. There are battles and boundaries that are necessary and those that are not. Forcing Drew to wear something to make *me* happy, when it made him so unhappy, was never a battle worth having. I suggested many times; however, that he might want to buy a new dress in a style of his own choosing, but he would just look at me, roll his eyes, and insist there was no such thing.

The girls reminded me why I was there.

"We saw Drew. What happened? Is he OK? He got here and we were so happy to see him and Kristin was giving him a hug and then the principal came over and made us go inside."

One of the girls told me she texted Drew and he told her he got kicked out. I was back on my mission.

"Have a wonderful time tonight, girls. If you don't have plans after the dance, feel free to come to our house and hang out with Drew and Mike."

I made my way over to the principal, introduced myself (although he knew who I was) and politely asked if he could explain what happened when Mike and Drew came to the dance.

"They are not students here. They are not enrolled. I asked them to leave. They didn't have tickets and they are not students here."

He must have sensed from the look on my face how his response had enraged me because before I could speak he added, "They were not dressed properly. And the students were required to sign up in advance so that we had enough food."

I remained calm although I wanted to strangle the man. Was he serious?

"First of all, my child *is* a student and has been a student in this district since kindergarten. He is enrolled, but he is on home-bound instruction and I believe you know why he is homebound. He did not sign up in advance, but couldn't you have made an exception? You could have simply asked him not to eat any of the food so that there is enough for the students that did sign up. And they may not have been dressed up in semi-formal attire, but the kids were neatly dressed. There are plenty of children in this district who cannot afford a boutique dress or suit. Did you make them leave? I just don't understand why you would exclude them from this opportunity to celebrate the end of middle school with their friends. Don't you know why Drew is homebound? Don't you understand what it means for him to have been able to come here?"

He became agitated with me, which really perplexed me because I thought I was being very calm and polite, hiding my distress. The momma bear in me wanted to tell him what I thought of him, but I held back. There were students and other teachers around. I didn't want to make a scene.

He said, "There is nothing I can do. Rules are rules and they are not enrolled students, they did not sign up in advance and they were not properly dressed. If I break the rules for one then I'd have to break the rules for anybody who just showed up at the door."

*Bullshit. You're the principal and you are the one who chose to enforce those rules. You could just as easily have chosen to make an exception and extend a kindness, especially to a straight-A student who has never been in trouble and who you know is battling depression and social anxiety.* I wanted to scream these words out loud, but I didn't. I'm not sure how the conversation ended, but I recognized fairly early that it wasn't going to accomplish anything. I learned what I came there to learn. It was not a misunderstanding—the principal was being an ass.

It was good that I had to walk home because I needed to calm down and collect my thoughts. How dare he? Did that really just happen? At the time, none of us knew the cause of Drew's depression and anxiety, only that it was so severe that he had attempted suicide three months earlier. I would expect the principal to have compassion. Hell, I would expect him to bend over backward and extend a very kind welcome when Drew walked in the door. I had never met a teacher or administrator who didn't genuinely care about the well-being of their students. This man didn't seem to have an ounce of empathy.

For a few minutes my child was happy to see his friends and they were excited to see him. For the first time in months Drew was at a social event with other teens. This was a straight-A student who had never been in trouble, ever. Why would he kick him out?

There are certain professions, particularly in the field of education, where people are looked upon as a role model. No matter what is going on, you check your personal life at the door. When you show up to work, you are expected to be at your best, most compassionate, supportive, accommodating self and be able to look beyond the immediate situation. This principal missed the boat that day. He had the opportunity to support a struggling student and contribute to a positive experience. Instead he embarrassed my child in front of the few friends he had and reinforced feelings that the middle school bullies had pounded into Drew—that he was a freak and a loser and would never fit in.

I can look back on this situation now, years later, and come up with many rational excuses for the principal's behavior. He's a human being. He probably had a lot on his mind. He had 150 other kids to keep in line; he didn't need two more. Still, I can't help but wish that evening had a different ending. I can't help but wish that instead of enforcing his rules, he might have decided to bend them and be a hero to a child who needed one.

---

### The Role of a Therapist

Throughout this book, we acknowledge several professionals who have had extensive experience with the problems we've encountered, as well as others, who are just good at what they do. Our experience with experts has generally been very good. However, we had to be careful that we, as parents, did not drive or inaccurately bias the process since many times it was a one-sided conversation without our son.

A good therapist is crucial. Our therapist provided objective, professional knowledge of human behavior, recognizing good and bad patterns in our family. We were too close to our problems to always see them. Even when we saw our problems; although we were smart, we didn't always have the knowledge and experience to apply the best solution. Our therapist provided that knowledge and experience.

It can take a long time to see the benefits from therapy. We were all entrenched in bad habits, limiting beliefs, and the extreme emotions brought up by our circumstances. It didn't help that we were all very stubborn. It took years to get where we were; it took us years to get out of it. Trust, acceptance of the truth, and the perseverance to make things better develop on their own timetable and generally cannot be willed into existence.

In hindsight, therapy for us gave us insight and compassion for our children going through therapy. It was hard for us as adults. We were sometimes uncomfortable, embarrassed, and ashamed to tell (or hear) the truth. It's really difficult.

For instance, Vince went to one therapy session feeling very angry about Billy missing appointments when Vince had rearranged his schedule to make an appointment possible. Expecting to find backup with the therapist; he instead was confronted with his mistake. Knowing Billy didn't feel obligated to show up for appointments at this period in his life, why did Vince reschedule important things in *his* life and get mad at Billy? The solution was for Vince to only reschedule his life when he could accept the possibility of a no-show. Vince really hated being told it was his own fault for allowing the situation, but from that point on, Billy only missed a few important appointments or arranged for his own transportation. Vince didn't change his schedule unless he really didn't mind. Miraculously, the sun kept rising even though Vince took care of himself.

Our children also saw our example and commitment when we went to therapy ourselves. In our children's eyes, therapy is different from a support group. Our own therapy takes the focus off them, and it says something about us as parents. It says we acknowledge our role in the issues, and we are willing to work on our problems. Of course, that's what we do in support groups, too. However, the broad term "support group" can imply we are not a part of the issue, somebody else is—in this case our children.

There are many people who we can say provided something we absolutely needed to get where we are today. Vivian, our therapist, stands out in this special crowd ... to the point that I think everyone should have a therapist and one as special as Vivian.

Vivian was referred to us by a friend when we were in crises with our older son. So often is the case when you are in a parenting crisis that people have all sorts of advice you don't want. Somehow we heard the recommendation to see Vivian and we accepted our friend's offer to set it up. It may have been the single smartest thing we did. Vivian's gift was cutting through the crap while building trust and expressing compassion. She initially worked with us, then Billy, and ultimately Drew. We came to her with two fragile children with very different needs. She worked with us patiently over many years and gained not only our trust, but the trust of our children.

Drew was especially difficult because he was acting inward and kept his secrets closely guarded. Vivian coached us to let Drew lash out in anger because he held so much inside. I remember being so uncomfortable with the idea because at the time angry outbursts equated to disrespect and that wasn't acceptable in our home. Well, we followed her instructions and I was the first to bear the brunt of his first tiny fit. It was definitely counter-intuitive to allow the behavior, but Vivian was right, and over time, all of her advice led to breakthroughs just as they had with our oldest son. It makes me feel really warm to think about how much Vivian cares and the difference she has made.

Some people expect to get parenting advice from their therapist so they can go home and fix their kids. That was not the only reason we sought help. Therapy for us was learning and understanding that we truly do not control other people—including our kids. In turn, we learned to deal with the emotions it brings up when others' behavior impacts us. We also learned to define our boundaries and how to enforce them. We learned how to communicate effectively—with respectful honesty, and without expectation.

**Chapter 6**

# A Fresh Start

*The future depends on what you do today.*
*—Mahatma Gandhi*

In the summer between eighth and ninth grade, Terri and I took Drew to see a home for sale in a nearby community. It was somewhat of a whim, but it soon got serious. We had considered moving in the past. At one time we thought relocating might remove Billy from an environment contributing to his troubles, but ultimately, we dismissed it as not likely to change anything. Now, Billy was no longer living at home.

We contacted a realtor and the three of us, including Drew, really enjoyed the experience of looking for a house. The moving bug bit us hard and Drew was all into it. It was nice to have him engaged in something, and it was fun for us, too. We soon found a house we liked in a new school district.

The school staff was welcoming and worked with us to make sure Drew could begin ninth grade on the first day of school along with everyone else. Even though we wouldn't be closing until a couple weeks into the new school year, we drove a half hour each morning to wait at the new house so Drew could ride the bus with the other kids in our new neighborhood.

With the counseling of his therapist, Drew tried to start out at the new school as a "girlier girl" with a new hairdo including bangs that required flat ironing. He bought a new wardrobe of fashionable form-fitting clothes. He wanted to fit in better and avoid the teasing and bullying that occurred in middle school.

The medication he was taking for his earlier diagnosis of ADD caused him to lose 50 pounds. It was good for ADD and skinny jeans, but not so good for his vision, as we found out later.

Medications, in general, were a complicated issue for both our children. Here's a little story highlighting one unusual problem we encountered.

### Really, He's Color Blind?

It concerned me that Drew kept complaining about not being able to read signs and was using the excuse that he was color blind to explain problems with class assignments. Terri and I were pretty sure Drew could see colors when he was younger. Drew and I had invented an elementary school science fair experiment to test if dogs could see colors. I still don't know if our border collie, Missy, can see colors, but Drew knew what he was doing. He made colorful posters, which proved he could discern colors.

With all that had happened over the years between our two kids, I had thought that I had become accustomed to "seeing the obvious," particularly after spending a small sum of money to have someone very qualified explain the obvious to me. The ophthalmologist did some testing and indeed confirmed Drew was color blind. Here comes the funny part. The doctor was still skeptical because while color blindness occurs overwhelmingly in men, it affects less than .5 percent of women.

Upon further questioning, I disclosed the list of medications Drew was taking at the time, and then it clicked. I was talking to the wrong doctor.

I never thought to investigate the medications first. The ophthalmologist assured me that Drew's eyes were healthy except for the color blindness. He recommended that I should investigate the drug side effects and interactions. Duh? I should have known.

Sure enough, the color blindness eventually went away. This is by no means scientific, but Drew and Terri firmly believe that Drew's vision returned to normal after stopping the medication, Topamax. Drew was taking this drug to treat the migraines he developed from the ADD medication, after an MRI scan—a somewhat desperate length—confirmed that it wasn't a brain tumor causing his headaches.

This whole process of discovery—from the doctors to the tests to the medications—was hard on Drew. One doctor suggested in front of Drew that he might be on the autism spectrum or possibly bi-polar. I'm not judging the doctor. I'm just feeling compassion for how hard this must have been on Drew.

### Anxiety & Depression Creep Back

Drew successfully battled to control his social anxiety by attending school every day until after Christmas when it became an overwhelming, perpetual struggle. His absences were increasing and his make-up work was mounting.

Mornings were a nightmare. "Will he be able to go to school today?" became the big question. Before the end of the year, he would need homebound instruction again.

We dreaded calling the attendance office each morning. It stirred our fears and insecurities of being judged as bad parents. Kids are supposed to go to school. Regular attendance is crucial to success in education and life, right?

As parents, we agree it is our responsibility to ensure our child goes to school. For most kids, we agree there need to be rules set in place, but when you have a child with long-standing depression and anxiety, conventional discipline doesn't fit the bill. For us, it was a balancing act of gentle pressure and trusting Drew when he was insistent he should stay home. The illness is real. However, you don't go to the doctor's office and get a note each time. That's why it's frustratingly naive when some yahoo gets carried away and thinks parents should be fined or arrested for not making their kid go to school.

Despite our self-inflicted and unpleasant feelings of calling the attendance office, we were confident in our decisions not to send Drew to school on bad days.

Our older son dropped out of high school after tenth grade, but he has since gone on to college. Therefore, we knew that dropping out was not necessarily a recipe for failure. Billy turned his life around nicely—once we got out of his way and stopped dictating that there is one and only one right way to get through school. We weren't going to fall into that trap with Drew and be held hostage to the belief that performance in high school was critical. So, we got over the graduation thing and accepted that there are just some things we can't control. We did our best to support Drew intelligently.

## Making It Safe for Outbursts

Having Drew home now for school simultaneously aided mine and Terri's deliberate decision to listen and trust our son more. As we mentioned before, Billy acted out with all sorts of bad behavior to deal with his problems, but Drew acted inwardly. He was cutting, isolating himself, and he attempted suicide. With Billy, Terri and I circled the wagons and created boundaries. For a couple years with Billy, it was one destructive power struggle after another until the lessons of therapy and our support group took hold.

Drew may have turned inward in part because he didn't like what he saw with Billy, but truthfully, Billy and Drew had very different personalities from the beginning. We found ourselves now looking for and trying to make it safe for Drew to have the outbursts that we had worked so hard to stop with Billy. Drew's therapist encouraged us to just let them happen. She advised that it was a good thing for him to vent his frustration in this manner.

It was hard for me. I seemed to bear the brunt of the outbursts and criticism when they finally happened. It's not surprising; Drew and I didn't get along too well for a period. I'm sure I'm not the only dad with the gift of being able to annoy or piss off his kids. Amazingly, though, through these outbursts we all learned we could trust each other with our frustrations and issues. With trust came more mature expressions of frustration, which ultimately led to effective resolutions.

---

### Something Good about the Internet

Before Drew knew why he was different, he did what most kids in the Internet age do for every problem they face: they pose their questions online. The anonymity of the Internet let him ask questions about being a lesbian, suicide, and eventually being transgender, without the fear of asking someone in person. People were online, sharing their stories and advice. This is where angels were looking out for him.

Drew was in a very fragile state for a while. While I would never want to leave my son's fate in the hands of complete strangers, no matter how well-intending or qualified they might be, and despite all the monitoring, counseling, and support we were providing our son, we found ourselves in that situation anyway.

We sometimes look back to this time and we're horrified that our son was seeking input from the Internet. How ironic, too, since Drew did exactly what we do when we first become aware of a problem. I'm now very proud of him for acting so maturely. Yes, using the Internet can be dangerous and risky, but we might still be wallowing around in the dark if Drew hadn't taken some action on his own to figure things out.

Drew's online inquiries eventually led to the first crucial conversation where he came out to us that he was a lesbian. From this point on, we were able to have a conversation about Drew's sexuality and later his gender identity, which was the ultimate source of his pain.

The Internet provided pivotal allies for Drew. They acted compassionately, intelligently, and anonymously. Once the ice was broken, we soon found that we had other allies at school, in our therapist, at a great place called the Q Center, and in support groups like Families Anonymous and PFLAG.

## Online Lifeline

We were monitoring Drew's computer activity on occasions when we were concerned, as he later suspected. We found him posting questions to Yahoo! Answers.

On at least one occasion, Drew was suicidal. He was so depressed that he didn't want to go on. At that time, he wasn't sharing his thoughts or feelings with us, so it was a little tricky to help him without betraying how we discovered what he was thinking. We didn't want to close down a vital source of information. Thankfully, there were people who were reading his posts and responding with thoughtful, caring, loving advice. Some advice was the same as or better than what I would have said to him myself. Others said what I know his therapist might have said. He was getting a mix of counseling I'd hope any trusted teacher, adult, supportive person, or a trained person working on a suicide hotline would say. People online were encouraging him not to give up, to seek help, to trust his parents. They were sharing their own personal experiences to connect with Drew. They told him to talk to us about how he was feeling. I am so touched that there were people, strangers really, saying the things that we would've said if we had known and had the opportunity.

Those people who answered Drew's call were angels guarding his life. They didn't know who they were talking to; they don't know that they may have saved a life.

I have an an incredible appreciation for people who give of their own time to read and respond to somebody who is putting out a call for help—not knowing really anything about the person they are responding to—having no idea who they are, if the problem is even real or if it's just a hoax, but yet are still willing to invest their time.

"Yes!" is our answer to that haunting question that must go through our angels' minds, "Did I help?"

We are eternally grateful, and we promise to pay it forward.

With that said, it certainly scared me to find and read Drew's deepest secrets online. What I read gave me far more understanding of what he was going through than he ever shared with us. It scared me because I knew the potential; I knew how real it was. These were his unedited, unfiltered thoughts and emotions.

Whereas I was once worried and imagined the worst, Drew was now communicating and confirming my worst fears through the questions he posed online. Some may say that we should have taken away his computer or shut down his Internet access, but it never occurred to us to do that. We knew we couldn't force him to talk to us instead of strangers. He wasn't coming to us. He was scared and he was hurting. We closely monitored his online activity and consulted with his therapist about how best to respond, given the nature of what we uncovered and how we found it.

Of course, I feared that one of those people responding online might not offer loving, supportive advice, but I could not control that. It was clear from some responses that somebody had posted very destructive, negative, and hateful advice to the effect of … "Hey, just go ahead and end it, your life isn't worth living." A moderator must have removed the offending post, but the responses from others alluded to it being there at one point. We are grateful to the online community at that time for shutting down this horrible person who encouraged my son to just go ahead and kill himself. I'm thankful to the moderators, hosts, and patrons who see the need to remove and filter out the negative, dangerous responses.

Drew's friends were also watching him online, on other websites. Apparently, Drew would make comments about cutting or suicide on Facebook, too. Thankfully, he had a few good friends who recognized the seriousness of the situation. They did the right thing by going to their parents who, in turn, contacted us. There were many times when we would get phone calls in the middle of the night just letting us know, "Hey, Drew just said something you need to know … Is he okay? He sounds really upset." This was very helpful when he was isolating. He really could put on a different face for us and hide from us, both literally and figuratively. As much and as hard as we tried, we just couldn't be there 24 hours watching his every move. I don't even kid myself into thinking that would have helped, that might have just driven him further into desperation.

Again, we never thought to shut down Drew's computer access, but we did become more vigilant about monitoring his activity. We realized that it doesn't matter how much we love him. No matter how hard we tried to communicate and keep lines of communication open, we still didn't have that power to actually make him talk to us unless he wanted to talk to us. For a while the Internet was his lifeline to hope—and our lifeline to him.

*We were very lucky to find Drew's comments online because we generally respected Drew's privacy. We had already missed the clues that preceded his earlier suicide attempt. We know that the circumstances and the depression that cause these dark feelings make it very difficult to seek help directly, but that's the best approach. For anyone reading this who may be considering hurting themself, please reach out to a social worker, a counselor, a teacher, a friend, your family, or a hotline. Resist giving up or assuming somebody knows or is monitoring your online activity. Tell as many people as you have to in order to get the help you need. We all need help from time to time.*

### Chapter 7

# Coming Out

*It takes courage to grow up and become who you really are.*
*—E.E. Cummings*

We started to see signs that things might be getting better. Drew was interested in laser scar removal. He wanted to remove the many, large scars on his arm from cutting, so we gladly spent a small fortune trying to erase the painful act that marked his eighth grade depression and hopelessness. The physical results; however, were modest compared to the secret joy we felt when Drew first walked casually downstairs wearing a short-sleeve shirt. For us, this moment marked the end of a long-standing sadness hidden beneath long sleeves and hoodies.

### A Brave Essay

Continuing on that good note, Drew came out to us gradually, starting in the summer between ninth and tenth grade. He tells the story of how he first came out to us in a memoir written for a tenth grade English assignment. His memoir was titled, *Harry Potter Wasn't the Only One Who Lived in a Closet*. What can we say?

We're proud of him and grateful to have him as our son (funny as 'son' sounds when you read the essay below).

### *Harry Potter Wasn't the Only One*
### *Who Lived in a Closet*

*I'm gay, although it wouldn't be a total shocker to anyone who found out. I mean, I wore clothes from the boy's section and my older brother's hand-me-downs since the time I started choosing what I could wear. Any clothes I received as a present from family members I'd accept graciously like my parents taught me to, but later return. They would usually get replaced with an oversized T-shirt or some pants that would be at least two sizes too big. I did nothing with my hair, just hopped out of the shower, brushed it and headed to school. I never wore makeup, I still don't now. So pretty much the only thing I did for my "appearance" was shove a couple dryer sheets in my pockets so I'd at least smell nice. And instead of playing with Barbie, I was playing Pokemon or with Legos. At some point in my childhood I truly wondered if I was a boy.*

*I actually thought my parents already knew I was gay. Fifteen and never had a boyfriend? Not very likely for a straight girl in this generation. I guess I was just a little bit paranoid, but with good reason. My parents did have a past of going through the history on my computer. If they went through the history before I came out to them, they would most likely find:*

- *YouTube: How to Come Out To Your Parents*
- *eHow: How to Come Out of the Closet*
- *YouTube: My Coming Out Story*
- *YouTube: Tips on Coming Out*

*I think you probably get the gist of what I'm trying to say. My computer history was full of me preparing myself to come out to them. I had been trapped in the closet way too long.*

*Like I said, I thought they already knew, and that they just didn't want to ask. That's totally understandable, not wanting to ask someone if they're gay. Because, if they were wrong it could kill a teenager's self-esteem. As it turned out, they actually hadn't gone through my computer. They could just sort of tell. As most people know, I am a horrible liar, and they could always tell when I lied. When they would ask if I had a boyfriend, I'd reply with "No" in that "Please stop asking that" tone every time. They knew I wasn't lying to them. I am one of those teenagers who actually doesn't lie to their parents.*

*So how the real beginning of this story started was one day this summer. The whole house was candle lit, making a strange mix of all sorts of different smells, because the power had just gone out. There was a crazy storm outside, obviously the cause of the power outage. The wind was so rough outside, all the chairs were knocked down, and even the big umbrella on our table blew off. That umbrella was held down with at least fifteen pounds of metal, plus the table itself. Everything was dead. Cell phone, iPod, laptop, video games, and everything else battery operated. I was practically forced by nature to sit and talk to my parents. Jokingly, my mom said, "So, it's time for you to tell us your deepest, darkest secrets." She didn't know she was actually about to find one out.*

*I didn't have the courage to straight up say, "Mom, Dad, I'm a lesbian." I don't know why, I was convinced they already knew. So I went with the only other idea I could think of. "Let's play twenty questions and see if you can figure it out." Their first question was obvious, "Are you pregnant?" Besides that being what any teenager's parent would ask first, this was recently after my brother told my parents that his girlfriend was pregnant. The second question was equally obvious. "Are you doing drugs?" My brother is a recovering drug addict, and they knew we were both so alike that they had to check. After many more totally ridiculous questions I responded with a 'no' and rolled my eyes every time.*

*Finally they started getting closer. "Is it about a boy you like?" After I said no once again so blatantly, they seemed like they were starting to get what I wanted to tell them. I could see, even in the candlelight, their eyes told me that the next question was something that would not get the same response. "Is it about a girl you like?" I took a long pause. I felt like I had to say something, anything, but my mouth wouldn't let me speak. It was like walking out of the dentist's after getting a tooth pulled, when your entire face is numb from the novocaine. One of my parents decided to put an end to my long, awkward silence and asked, "Honey, do you like girls?" This time I opened my mouth to speak, but then knowing that was the point of this whole conversation, I shut it and just nodded. That was it. I was out.*

*My dad was raised Roman Catholic, my mom also raised in a Catholic home. I knew that they were no longer religious, only spiritual, but that didn't make those few seconds between when I nodded and when they spoke to me any less terrifying. Just a few short seconds of waiting felt like hours. What I had just done was going to change my life forever, and I didn't know whether that change would be good or bad. A whole lot of thoughts ran through my head, the majority of them not pleasant. I sort of came back to Earth once my mom started talking. She was pretty much going off on a speech on how there was "nothing wrong with that," and that "it's okay that I liked girls." I did spend the last several years trying to figure that out, she didn't need to tell me, but it did comfort me a bit. My dad could see on my face that I had already realized that, and told her she could stop. He said that they would both love me, no matter what, and that I didn't have to worry about being judged by them. Hearing those words felt like it lifted a stack of bricks off my chest. And suddenly, the power outage and the smell of mixed candles didn't seem quite as bad.*

## Finding the Q Center

When tenth grade began, Drew returned to the classroom rather than continue with homebound instruction. At this point, we knew he was a lesbian. We were hopeful that with our support, love, and acceptance, he would overcome some of his depression and anxiety and learn to love and accept himself.

Drew was subjected to some teasing and bullying again; this time it was because he came out as a lesbian. One person felt it was her religious duty to make Drew feel bad. The other was a bully seeking to elevate his self-esteem by picking on someone vulnerable. He was definitely feeling higher anxiety. It was hard for Drew to continue with school, but he did for a while.

During a meeting with Drew's guidance counselor, I shared that Drew was a lesbian. The counselor asked me if I knew about the Q Center, a place for lesbian, gay, bisexual and transgender (LGBT) youth. She gave me a brochure and when I got home, I called immediately to get information about the youth groups for kids Drew's age.

For more than three years, Drew didn't want to leave the house; you can imagine getting him to go to a youth group was a pretty tough sell. His self-inflicted, social isolation had been going on for several years. He didn't want to be around other kids. When he needed clothes, we went to a store an hour away to prevent the risk of running into anybody he knew. It wasn't just the kids at his school. He really didn't feel comfortable around any teens.

Initially, Drew was very resistant to the Q Center, but it turns out that the Q Center was open to allies and not just to LGBT youth. Drew reluctantly agreed to go if someone went with him. There were two friends who later went regularly with Drew, but the first time was the most pivotal. Including allies is something the Q Center really got right.

## Our Surprise

I will never forget the first time we dropped Drew off at the Q Center. The car ride there was quiet. He was really nervous. His friend didn't say anything, either. Once we were sure they were at the right place and got the "all OK" from him, we left them there—nothing more embarrassing than having your parents hover.

The group met for an hour and a half, but we went back twenty minutes early to be safe. From the parking lot we could see through the partially closed blinds. Drew was flitting about in there. He was laughing and interacting with the other kids. I remember the feeling in my heart. For that entire hour after we dropped him off, I kept thinking about how much he didn't want to go. He never wanted to go anywhere. To see him laughing—which we hadn't seen in years—made us cry.

When it got closer to the end of the meeting, I sent him a text to let him know we were in the parking lot. We were ready whenever he was ready. Suddenly, we could see in the window that he began hugging people. He was hugging people saying goodbye! There was a lot of hugging! Vince and I looked at each other, and we both had tears in our eyes.

From that point forward, he couldn't wait to go back. In addition to the regular meetings, it seemed like he was at every event and volunteered for every activity, including the Pride Parade and Equality and Justice Day in Albany. He would go early to set up and then stay late to help clean up.

The Q Center was such a huge change for him. The extreme social anxiety that caused him to be homebound from school for three years disappeared when he was at the Q Center. He found a place where he fit in and people accepted him openly. His sexuality and ultimately his gender identity didn't matter. He was just a kid getting to be a kid. It was probably the first time he was able to be a regular teenager. He could talk about music and video games; any and all of his interests. He was doing all of the things that kids his age do and most parents take for granted.

Over the next couple of months, through new friendships, support, and awareness, Drew could start to put words to the struggle still inside him.

### Drew Wasn't Done Coming Out

We were somewhat relieved when Drew came out as a lesbian. It answered a lot of questions. It gave us something concrete to work with besides chemically treating the host of mysterious psychological symptoms that plagued Drew for the past two years.

However, coming out as a lesbian was just one chapter in the evolution of the truth. First he thought he was bisexual. Then he thought he was a lesbian. Then he said he sometimes feels more like a boy than a girl. Then he said he feels like a boy more often than he feels like a girl. Finally, he came out and said, "I *AM* a boy."

The discovery was gradual. In part, he was getting comfortable and testing our reactions to see if it was safe. Would we accept him? Would we still love him? But we also know now that he was still figuring out who he was and coming to terms with his identity himself. He was still fighting it and trying to be someone he wasn't. He was trying so hard to live a conventional life, to fit in, and to not be different. Nobody decides to be transgender. They decide what they are going to do about it.

The story doesn't end with Drew declaring he's transgender and everybody—including Drew—is fine with it. But it was the first step with a long journey still ahead. If you are already familiar with gender identity and sexual orientation, you can see Drew was blending two separate issues. We'll talk about the distinction between gender identity and sexual orientation in a later chapter. It's important to understand the difference.

---

### A True Friend and Ally

Not long after Drew proclaimed he was a boy, I shared the new information with a good friend. Vince and I have known Christine for many years. Drew has been friends with Christine's daughter since before kindergarten. We've shared many activities together over the years, including spending a week at Disney World shortly after Drew's suicide attempt.

Earlier in our friendship when Billy's situation was overwhelming, Christine was so compassionate and supportive. She has no idea how much her friendship helped. Christine referred us to our therapist, Vivian, whom she so highly recommended, that we were able to let go of our pride and insecurities to actually make an appointment.

Amazingly, when I shared with Christine that Drew was transgender, she knew exactly what I was talking about. Christine had recently attended a work conference where one of the speakers was a transgender woman named Donna Rose. Christine shared that experience with me and the same evening let me borrow Donna Rose's book, *Wrapped in Blue*. I read it right away. Vince would secretly read Donna's book when I put it down, and he credits the book with starting his serious acceptance of Drew's gender identity.

Christine was the first person I told about Drew. I felt scared and alone. I didn't have a very good understanding of gender identity disorder or the terminology behind it. Christine made me feel safe and understood my anxiety. She even said that she had long suspected Drew was transgender. What a blessing to talk with Christine for my first "coming out" story. Yes, parents have to come out, too. It was a very positive and encouraging event.

Christine and her daughter continued to alert us about Drew's online activity. During the darkest hours of Drew's depression, he would write something online that signaled trouble. Drew's friend would tell her mom and then Christine would call to alert me. Sometimes we received calls after midnight. I can only imagine how hard it is to make a call like that, but they did it more than once and we are very grateful.

With so much behind us now, Vince and I look back with admiration on Christine's example. She is a true friend and ally.

# Chapter 8

## Converging on the Truth

*It is time for parents to teach young people early on that in diversity there is beauty and there is strength. We all should know that diversity makes for a rich tapestry, and we must understand that all the threads of that tapestry are equal in value no matter their color.*

—Maya Angelou

One night Drew came to me frightened, desperate, broken. It was a look that was all too familiar to me. A look that I knew would require my full attention and support. He needed his mom, he needed to be heard, and he needed to trust that I would know what to do. He said six powerful words: "I need to be someplace safe."

Midway through tenth grade, Drew had begun living at home and at the Q Center as a male. He was back to wearing men's clothing and got his hair cut short. We were using male pronouns and his preferred name "Drew" instead of his birth name. Although he wasn't out as a male to anyone outside our family or the Q Center, he could feel things already starting to turn around and get better.

He felt ready to share his identity with others.

Others; however, were not as accepting and understanding. Life started to feel overwhelming again. He felt that no one really saw him as a guy—and he feared they never would. It began to take its toll on him. Even with countless hours of therapy and numerous medications, his anxiety wasn't getting any better. It became too much for him to handle.

Drew had given up hope and felt he'd rather die than continue the struggle. Thankfully, he recognized this emotional place and what he was contemplating. He remembered the key words to say when he came to me that night. "I need to be someplace safe." I knew exactly what he meant. After a quick consult with Drew's therapist, I had a plan.

I let Vince know what was going on, and then I took Drew to the pediatric emergency room at Golisano Children's Hospital. Vince and I both knew not to argue when Drew said he felt more comfortable going with just mom.

It was a miracle break-through that Drew was able to come to us at all. I don't know if this was Drew's first suicidal ideation since his attempt nearly two years earlier, but this is exactly what we wanted to happen when the thoughts came back. Drew was fighting along with us, not hiding from us.

Hospital and social workers will want to pay attention here.

Golisano Children's Hospital got it right. The human experience there was life-changing for Drew, as well as for Vince and me. We learned over the next few days (and weeks) how important it was to embrace the discovery process that was going on within Drew. We, as parents, would watch our child truly open up. Finally.

A social worker assigned to take care of Drew was an angel in disguise. She performed the intake interview and assessed Drew's state and reason for feeling suicidal. Drew looked to me to answer the questions that were difficult for him. I fumbled for the right words as I tried to explain that although Drew is a girl, he feels more like a boy than a girl. I explained that he had been living as a boy at home for more than a month but had just started expressing himself this way to a few friends and others outside our home.

The social worker knew all about transgender youth. She was so supportive and knowledgeable. She immediately "got" the male pronouns and called Drew by his preferred name. Drew was visibly relieved that we got to speak with someone who actually knew what he was talking about. Soon he relaxed and answered questions himself, rather than look to me. For me, it was so comforting, consoling, and satisfying to see that my son was able to speak and be heard, when the person he was speaking to was able to see him and affirm who he really was. Who knew we would find an ally like this in an emergency room?

Vince and I had never used the name "Drew" outside of our home before. I was uncomfortable and fearful of how this would all play out. This particular social worker was one of many allies and angels placed along our path to help us. She informed the rest of the staff of Drew's preferred name and pronoun usage, and the staff took it very seriously. I didn't have to educate anyone who interacted with Drew and be the corrector of pronouns—an experience that always made Drew shrink and withdraw. I didn't have to advocate for my son with every new nurse and doctor who saw him. Instead, I was free to just be Drew's mom.

Drew responded well and things improved quickly. It was the first time Drew was actually accepted by the outside world and it seemed to give him hope. He was delighted to hear his name, a name he had chosen. I remember the friendly staff person who would arrive with his breakfast tray and cheerfully say, "Good morning, Andrew. It's going to be a good day today. I hope you enjoy your breakfast!" The lab technicians who collected Drew's blood, the nurses who tended to him day and night, even the kind men and women who cleaned his room and emptied his trash— they all called him Andrew and used male pronouns.

It's important to note that the actions of the doctors and staff conveyed the message that a respected authority acknowledges and validates the basic transgender human condition. Up until this point, validation had only come to us from the Internet, the Q Center, and books.

For Vince and me, it was a pivotal time to watch others affirm our son—using his preferred name and male pronouns. We were able to observe the effect it had on Drew. He arrived at the hospital feeling hopeless, thinking the world would never accept him for who he was, and wanting to end his life because it was too hard to pretend to be somebody he was not. He arrived shaking, crying, head down, and unable to look even me in the eye. I watched the tension, fear, and pain disappear as Drew began to relax. It paralleled his first day at the Q Center.

As we observed Drew's reaction toward the simple acts of others affirming him, we realized that our job as parents extended far beyond providing a safe home. It required us to support him in getting to a place where others would see and know him as a male. He needed to be who he truly is, and we needed to help make that happen.

In a private conversation, the social worker told me about her experience in Philadelphia working with transgender youth. Her words added an ingredient to my growth; she validated what I already knew intuitively—that my son's condition was very real and very serious—but there was also help and hope. She told me about an annual conference in Philadelphia that provided comprehensive education on transgender issues, free of charge.

Drew spent four days at Golisano Children's Hospital waiting for a bed to become available at a nearby psychiatric hospital. We were insistent that Drew be sent to Four Winds; a healthcare facility we were already familiar with and personally give two thumbs up.

The trip there was an uncomfortable three-hour ambulance ride, but I was grateful I could ride with Drew. It's a surreal experience to sit in an ambulance with my son and look back through the rear window to see Vince, alone and following in our car. Two years earlier, Vince and I were following Billy in the ambulance after Billy's suicide attempt. I remember the worry and hopelessness we felt on that long and silent ride. As I looked back at Vince, I thought how lonely and scared he must feel. I looked down at Drew who was lying with his head in my lap, holding my hand, and thought he, too, must feel lonely and scared. *We will get through this*, I thought. *Four Winds helped Billy, it will help Drew.*

The intake experience at Four Winds was just as we had expected. Adam, the therapist who interviewed the three of us not long after we arrived, was knowledgeable and skillful when asking Drew questions. Drew was open and engaged in the conversation. I smiled inside.

While at Golisano's, Vince coached Drew to be an active participant in his own health and wellness. Vince used the example of Drew's last pair of eye glasses. Drew had noted how good his prescription was. Vince pointed out that the lenses were so good because Drew took his eye examination seriously—something only he could do. Drew's previous glasses lacked visual clarity because an impatient Drew didn't see the importance of taking the time to select the correct lens during the exam.

Drew took the advice and was now vested in the process at Four Winds. Adam also made it easy. He was able to relate with Drew, interpret his feelings, and repeat them back accurately. Their dialogue was genuine, honest, and clear. It was fascinating to watch.

In the past, Drew would become so frustrated whenever Vince and I tried to verbalize what we thought he was feeling. I think it pleased Drew that we could be there to witness the discourse between him and Adam, to see it firsthand.

Over the course of his two-week stay, Drew was feeling validated, and I too walked away with a new confidence, building on the experience at Golisano Children's Hospital.

It was hard for me and Vince to accept that we couldn't help Drew ourselves. We had to depend on experts outside our family, just as we had with Billy. We did the best we could to select the professionals, programs, and facilities to help us and our children, but ultimately, we had to turn it over to the experts and let go. The Serenity Prayer reminds us of this every day as we pray for the serenity to accept the things we cannot change, courage to change the things we can, and the wisdom to know the difference.

We left Four Winds with something we didn't expect or even know was a possibility—a formal diagnosis of Gender Identity Disorder (GID), the term used by psychologists and physicians to describe persons who experience significant gender dysphoria (discontent with the sex they were assigned at birth and/or the gender roles associated with that sex). It was as if Drew became officially transgender. For me and Vince, it was certainly easier to explain to people now that we had a formal, medical diagnosis.

The DSM-V, the newest edition of the psychiatric diagnostic manual, which was released in May 2013, stopped labeling transgender people as "disordered." The DSM-V replaced the diagnostic term, "gender identity disorder," with the term, "gender dysphoria." Based on standards set by the DSM-V, individuals will now be diagnosed with gender dysphoria for displaying, "a marked incongruence between one's experienced/expressed gender and assigned gender."

Drew never returned to his classes after he came home from Four Winds. The high school graciously provided homebound instruction for the remainder of tenth grade.

Drew continued to attend the regular LGBT youth meetings at the Q Center, but also began attending the monthly TransYouth group meetings. These sessions taught Drew about gender identity and how it is completely different from sexual orientation. He also got to know many other transgender youth just like him.

After an initial meeting at the Q Center, Drew told us about an interaction with a guy he met there. Drew had asked if the guy used to be a girl. This was back before he knew the language and what was appropriate, offensive, or insensitive. Now, the notion 'used to be a girl' doesn't make sense or even sound right.

The Q Center is a safe space and Drew's language problem was overcome with time. What's great is that the Q Center has programming that helps kids learn the vocabulary and facts. Drew finally started connecting the dots in his life. We did, too.

Although he had always felt like a boy, Drew was able to live with a female body because it wasn't an issue before puberty. In his mind, he was attracted to more boyish things. He always wore male clothes. It was never a big deal. When puberty hit, the problem then became acute because now things were happening that definitely contradicted his sense of who he was. His body was changing and betraying him. Drew realized that he was transgender.

Gradually, Vince and I made friends with adults at the Q Center. We found it was a safe place for us, too. LGBT, much less transgender, was all new to us. It was scary in a "fear of the unknown" sort of way. The parents, staff, and volunteers at the Q Center were excellent supports for us. After Drew came out as transgender, we started attending the TransParent group at the Q Center, a support group for parents of transgender and gender non-conforming youth.

At our first TransParent meeting, we met Karen and Jason. What struck me about this couple was how much they embraced their child and their child's gender identity. They were quintessential role models. They taught us how far we could go, how supportive we could be, and how important it is to advocate for your child. Their relationship with their child was beautiful. A lot of our fears and uncertainty were counterbalanced by Karen and Jason's positive experience. We saw a place of normalcy and true acceptance in our future—hope beyond our current fears of the unknown.

Months later, when the Q Center's program coordinator left the area, Karen and I became co-leaders of the TransParent group—a responsibility we still share. I am committed to being there for other parents, as Karen and others had been there for me. For a while our group was very small, but it has since steadily grown.

The Q Center has played an important role in our lives, providing a safe place for our son while serving as a catalyst for our own growth. While connecting us with friends and resources, the Q Center also merges merriment and a playful spirit. A beautiful example of this is the Pride Prom, a formal dance put on each year by the Q Center.

At the Pride Prom, kids can attend with whomever they want. If a guy wants to bring a guy, he brings a guy. If a girl wants to bring a girl, she brings a girl. They can wear whatever they want and express their identity. Many kids find their high school dances restrictive and intolerant. Recall before Drew's transition, he was not allowed to enter a dance because he didn't wear a dress.

In the three years Drew has been attending the Q Center, we have seen that the kids really look forward to the Pride Prom. It's a very good thing. Drew's first experience was priceless.

When Drew first told us about the prom, he asked if he could get a suit. This was after years of never wanting to go shopping for clothes. I remember the moms of Drew's friends often telling me how lucky I was that my child didn't live at the mall and didn't constantly beg me to take him shopping for new clothes, shoes, jewelry, make-up, and hair accessories. Don't get me wrong, I believe in expressing and being grateful for what you have, rather than dwelling and yearning for what you don't have. However, it never felt right to be grateful that Drew avoided malls. It wasn't that he was content with what he had; rather, he was hiding from the world. I always felt like we were missing a normal, healthy experience with our teenager.

So here I was being presented with a request to get a suit. And what did we do? We went shopping! I cried in JC Penney. Drew was trying on suits and having so much fun. He would come out of the changing room and look at himself proudly in the three-way mirror. He modeled and showed himself off. He was really excited. He struck pose after pose and just strutted around, "Hmmm, should I wear a vest? Let me try this vest on. I think I like this vest. Should I do suspenders?" He loved what he saw in the mirror, and so did I.

I was crying because for years Drew wouldn't look in a mirror. He hated the mirror. He had such dysphoria; what he saw in the mirror caused him such pain. It makes sense now because someone presenting as a girl was reflecting back at him and this was not what he felt like inside. When he saw himself in a suit, the guy in the mirror finally matched what he felt inside. He liked what he saw. He saw a guy trying on all these different suits and it felt right. By the way, he looks darn good in a suit!

I can't say the excursion all went perfectly, though. Drew still had a female body. Unlike a male's body, he was curvy, and his shorter stature made it more difficult to find pants that fit him right. Drew wore a binder to flatten and conceal his chest. His binder showed through some of the shirts he tried on, so he had to make adjustments. Overall, however, it was a joyful day—especially for the mom who had been waiting fifteen years for an occasion like this!

Fast forward to prom night when Vince and I dropped off Drew. The prom was at a hall in an unfamiliar part of town, but we were learning to let go and trust more. We appreciated how the staff at the Q Center knows how vulnerable the kids are and they are very protective. We returned to pick Drew up just before the prom was about to end. We texted him so that he knew we were waiting. We saw him saying his goodbyes, hugging at least twenty people. What parent's heart wouldn't be warmed by such a sight?

As he walked toward the car, I watched him. I was just fascinated. He seemed so relaxed, confident, and happy. Could this be the same boy that was so broken only a few short months ago? The boy who couldn't hold his head up, couldn't look anyone in the eye? Now, he walked tall and proudly.

I looked a bit more closely. He had a crown. I remember asking Vince, "Do you see that? He's got a crown. What do you think that crown means? Why's he wearing a crown? Are they all wearing party hats?" I looked around thinking they just put party hats on, but nobody else was wearing a hat or a crown. "What do you think the crown means?" He also had all these beads around his neck. He had so many beads it looked like Mardi Gras. He had so many, you would think he would fall over. The other kids didn't have the beads. What was up with that?

He and a friend finally got in the car. Half-jokingly, but silently hoping, I had to ask, "So what's the crown? Are you prom king?" Drew said, "Yeaaaah!" and got this big smile on his face.

I later learned the prom organizers gave each of the youth two strings of beads when they arrived at the prom. They were each instructed to put one strand around the neck of the person they chose as prom king and one around the neck of the person they chose for prom queen.

I let my understanding of what had happened sink in. All of those beads around my son's neck had been placed there by his friends; by the dozens of peers in attendance who chose him to be their prom king.

It's painful to think back to the time when he was so lost and alone. He didn't have many friends. He didn't want to be around anybody. Now, he was voted prom king by his friends and other kids he met there that night. I still get a warm flood of goosebumps when I think of that moment. As a mom, I am overcome with feelings of love and gratitude for those young people at the prom who lifted up my son when they placed their beads around his neck, and to the many allies and angels who led us to this place.

---

### What is Transgender?

When Vince and I first learned that our son's years of depression and anxiety might stem from an inner struggle with his gender identity, I rushed to learn all I could. I performed Google searches, watched and read personal accounts of transgender people, sought transgender studies, read every book I could get my hands on, and consulted with doctors, professionals and experts. Here's what I found.

Essentially, transgender people challenge traditional ideas about gender and defy social expectations of how they should look, act, or identify, based on their birth sex. Transgender is an umbrella term used to encompass individuals, behaviors, and groups whose gender identity or gender expression do not conform to society's expectations of what it means to be male or female. Many identities fall under the transgender umbrella, including transsexuals, cross dressers, drag queens and drag kings.

Transgender is often shortened to trans. Trans or trans* is an abbreviation that began as a way to be more inclusive or concise in reference to the different identities that could be referenced by using the term. The asterisk implies that trans* encompasses transgender, transsexual, and other transitional identities challenging the gender binary.

Transsexuals are people who experience an intense, persistent, and long-term feeling that their body and assigned sex do not match their gender identity. Such individuals desire to change their bodies to bring them into alignment with their gender identities.

The term transsexual comes from the medical establishment and many people do not like this term. I've been told it can be an "ouch" word and is not a term I should impose on people. However, there are some people who prefer the term transsexual, such as my son.

As I tried to understand all I was reading, my head was spinning. There was a lot of terminology, much of which didn't make sense to me at the time, and some of which made me uncomfortable.

At first, I got hung up on phrases like, "challenging traditional ideas" and "defying social expectations," because to me, those words implied a *chosen* behavior of an individual to defy or rebel against society. This clearly was not a chosen behavior on my son's part. I know this and I can tell you this with absolute certainty that he did not choose to be trans—nobody would deliberately choose such a hard life in our society.

At awareness training and workshops, we often start out by explaining the difference between sexual orientation and gender identity, and then define each of the following separately: birth sex, gender identity and gender expression. When these terms were broken down for me, it became easier to understand and explain them to others.

Before expounding further, I'm going to oversimplify in a non-scientific, non-textbook way just as somebody once explained to me. They said, "Terri, your child has a male brain inside of a female body."

Many of us think "penis = boy and vagina = girl." Most of the time this turns out to be the case, but not always.

Numerous studies have confirmed the long-held suspicion about the brains of males and females. They're not the same. Scientists now know that sex hormones begin to exert their influence during development of the fetus. I won't bore you with the studies and the brain imaging technology used to capture and analyze the differences, but if you want to confirm for yourself, the findings are out there.

What I had always assumed; however, was that a penis and a male brain came as a matched set, just like a vagina and a female brain were supposed to be a matched set. It does not always turn out that way.

A child can be born with a variety of unexpected, uncommon or undesirable traits. For example, an extra finger or missing toe. Similarly, a child can be born with missing organs, a malformed heart, an undescended testicle, a missing testicle, or a variety of other unusual traits, which some may call "birth defects." I personally don't like to imply that being born transgender is a birth defect, although my son refers to his condition as a birth defect. I respect that certain terminology can influence reactions—what may be offensive to some can be acceptable to others—and I offer this example with the hope that it helps clarify my point.

My child was born with a male brain inside of a female body. There are different theories and studies that explain why and how this happens. Briefly, some believe a hormone imbalance during fetal development causes an individual's gender identity (what is in their brain) to not match their biological sex (what is between their legs.)

At first, these concepts of mismatched gender identity and biological sex were difficult for me to grasp because I had always lived in a body that was aligned with how I identified. When I was born, I had a vagina and I was labeled a girl. This wasn't a problem because I always felt "like a girl," dressed "like a girl," acted "like a girl" and was happy to be a girl. My sex and gender identity were a matched set. They were aligned. For most of the population, our sex and gender identity are aligned, so this can be a challenging concept to comprehend.

I committed my time and energy to understand so I could best support my son. The reality is I could spend a lifetime studying the causes, diagnostic criteria, and variations, but I had to make decisions now. There was enough information and research to convince me that being transgender was a legitimate condition.

What is someone's sex? What is someone's gender? What is the difference between sex and gender? Think in terms of what we're born with versus what we learn. Everyone is born with a birth sex, and everyone develops a gender identity.

It is helpful to grasp a couple key concepts:

- The distinction between birth sex, gender identity and gender expression, and

- The distinction between sexual orientation and gender identity.

## Birth Sex

Your birth sex could be male, female, or intersex (having both female and male sexual characteristics). A label of male or female is assigned at birth based on the appearance of external genitalia, and this is the sex designation that appears on birth certificates and other legal documents. Chromosomes are another way of labeling birth sex, although most of us don't have our chromosomes tested and verified at birth. A child born with a penis is assigned the birth sex male (and is assumed to have two distinct sex chromosomes, XY.) A child born with a vagina is assigned the birth sex female (and is assumed to have two X chromosomes.) Intersex people have various combinations of sex chromosomes, hormone levels, and genitalia.

Birth sex refers to the physiological and anatomical characteristics that a person is born with or that develop with physical maturity, including internal and external reproductive organs, chromosomes, hormones, body shape, and genitals. Birth sex is also referred to as "assigned sex" or "biological sex."

## Gender Identity

Your gender identity is your internal sense of being male, female or gender non-binary. Gender identity is "between your ears" whereas birth sex is "between your legs."

Gender identity, a person's own understanding of themselves in terms of categories like boy or girl, man or woman, transgender and others, is how a person feels inside—what they believe themselves to be.

An individual understands their gender identity much earlier than their sexuality. By ages two and three, children begin noticing the difference between being a boy and being a girl, and they start to identify with one or the other. Some studies show gender-typed play begins as early as eighteen months.

## Gender Expression

Gender expression is behaviors and lifestyle choices that convey something about a person's gender identity, or that others interpret as meaning something about their gender identity, including clothing, hairstyle, mannerisms, communication patterns, social roles, etc. We often categorize gender expression as being masculine, feminine, or androgynous.

Your DNA doesn't determine how you style your hair or what clothes you like to wear.

Gender expression is not binary (that is, it is neither exclusively masculine nor feminine) and it is not necessarily aligned with birth sex or gender identity. For example, a man can be masculine or feminine just as a woman can be masculine or feminine. Furthermore, all people can fall somewhere on the spectrum between masculine and feminine, and where they fall can change from day to day.

## Sexual Orientation

Your sexual orientation equates to your physical, sexual and/or romantic attraction to others. It is who you are attracted to or who you love. Sexual orientation describes an enduring pattern of attraction and the inclination or capacity to develop intimate, emotional, and sexual relationships with other people. Sexual orientation is usually quantified in terms of gender—both an individual's own gender and the gender(s) of the people to whom that person is attracted to. Categories for sexual orientation include straight, gay, lesbian, bisexual, queer, pansexual, asexual, and questioning, among many others. These categories, like all of this terminology, are constantly evolving.

I ask you to break away from what might be a tendency to look at birth sex, gender identity, gender expression, and sexual orientation as binary—that somebody is either male or female, a man or a woman, masculine or feminine, straight or gay. The components of sexual and gender identity are not binary and are not easily defined by checking one of only two boxes, although many of us have been conditioned to view them as binary.

I also ask you to consider that the components just discussed (birth sex, gender identity, gender expression, and sexual orientation) are not aligned or associated with each other in any particular groupings. One should not assume that a person born male would naturally identify as a man, be masculine, and be attracted to women. Likewise, one should not assume a person born female would identify as a woman, be feminine, and be attracted to men. For cultural, political, religious, and personal reasons some might want this to be true, but it does not match the reality of the human population. Men and women can be masculine, feminine or somewhere in between. A man can be attracted to men or women or both, and a woman can be attracted to men or women or both. A person can be born male but identify as a woman and vice versa.

The diagram below indicates many, but not all, of the possibilities.

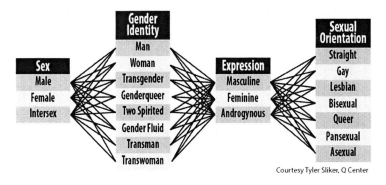

Courtesy Tyler Sliker, Q Center

# Chapter 9

# Turning Point as Parents

*As I considered my story, I found an odd paradox: that the power of the story came from the depth of the self-disclosure.*
—*Donna Rose*

**D**rew had been patient with therapy, testing medications for depression and anxiety, and allowing us, as his parents, to help him. When Drew began to seriously consider and ultimately accepted that he is transgender, Vince and I owed it to him to educate ourselves on what being transgender means.

It wasn't easy, though. We had the same limiting beliefs many people have, who have never heard of or met a transgender person. Remember the questions from our introduction:

*How could a child know who they are or what they want at that age?*

*What kind of parent could let their child do something like that?*

*I don't care what age the person is, that's wrong.*

As parents on this journey, it was vital to separate the outside world and our own insecurities from our child's needs. For a period of time, we insulated ourselves from the harsh judgmental voices of others. We didn't need their skeptical, fearful commentary influencing us. Although we were also ignorant about gender identity disorder, we knew it would do no good to listen to their input—no matter how well-intentioned they might seem. We needed to immerse ourselves in research, as well as consult doctors and experienced specialists. Allowing Drew to live safely as a male in our home throughout this process was a huge step toward discovering and affirming his gender for ourselves.

We had three key questions about being transgender. The first was, "Can this actually happen where the biological sex does not match gender identity?" When we understood and accepted that this mismatch actually happens, we had to ask the next question, "Can a child know he is transgender at age fifteen?" Again, when we were satisfied that, yes, a child's gender identity is formed in the first few years of life, the next question was, "How do we know if *our* child is transgender and needs to transition for a happy, healthy life?" After all, not every gender non-conforming child is transgender or needs to transition.

Vince and I are engineers. We're the geeky, logical, fact-driven, list-making, science-oriented types, and we dove into these questions looking for solid answers. Silently, I prayed that we would find something to disprove what I intuitively knew was true. I was hoping that I would find an answer amidst the research that would let me keep my little girl.

*God, let it be anything else. I can handle and support my child through anything, but please not this. How will he get through this? How will I?* These thoughts consumed me.

We didn't want this. We went through the stages—from shock to denial to damage control, and finally to acceptance. In hindsight, gaining a son is a beautiful thing and we are grateful and know how lucky we are to have him. But for a time, we grasped desperately to the child we thought we were losing.

Our research and professional consultations gave us the answers and confidence we needed to know what we had ultimately come to accept—that our son was transgender. It was real, and in our son's case, transition was urgent. We needed to move forward.

While we had the medical and scientific answers we needed, it was the Donna Rose book, *Wrapped in Blue*, that gave us emotional insight. Donna Rose demystified what it meant to be transgender. Her words helped me to understand her feelings and her experience living in the wrong body. I could feel her pain—not just the pain of being a woman trapped in a man's body, but the pain from years of trying to deny it, trying to be somebody she wasn't, and trying not to hurt the people she loved. Her bravery in telling such a personal story is commendable. I'm grateful for her courage because her words helped me better understand what my son was feeling. It helped me better understand my role in either perpetuating or alleviating my son's pain.

Donna Rose revealed her struggles in a way that I was able to connect with her as a real person every bit as deserving of love and compassion as anybody else. That connection enabled me to see through my social, educational, and other filters, and ultimately see gender identity as separate from one's genitalia.

We are in a time of increasing acceptance of transgender people, but it wasn't always that way; *Wrapped in Blue* encapsulated the choice before me, as a parent of a transgender son. Donna Rose missed out on a significant portion of her life as a woman because family and social norms didn't provide for transition during her childhood. I soon learned that many transgender children do not survive to be adults. I became committed to supporting my son's transition. I didn't want him to miss another day of living his life, comfortable in his own skin.

Perhaps the most important lesson I learned from Donna Rose was how it feels to be transgender and not be able to express your identity freely. I developed the compassion and empathy that I'm embarrassed Vince and I didn't have from the beginning.

We became more committed to putting aside our fears and reaching out. A friend suggested we attend a chapter meeting of PFLAG, the original ally organization founded in 1972, which advocates in various ways for the LGBT community.

Walking into my first PFLAG meeting, I felt nervous. Who would be there and would I fit in? I was afraid I'd be judged. I was afraid that nobody at the PFLAG meeting would have any experience with a transgender child. Surely everybody there would be families and friends of lesbians and gays—after all, PFLAG stands for Parents, Families and Friends of Lesbians and Gays. Was I going to have to educate everybody at the meeting about what it means to be transgender and the challenges our family had been encountering?

If Vince was nervous, he didn't show it. He accompanied me to this meeting. We were supporting each other as we always have throughout our entire marriage. Vince is always strong, even when he is as scared and as clueless as I am.

It took all of about thirty seconds before I realized I was in the right place; I was accepted, warmly welcomed, and understood. Being at this PFLAG meeting was like being at my first Families Anonymous meeting. I was in a room full of people just like me. Although all of our stories were different, we shared a common, deep love for our children, and an understanding of the difficult challenges they faced. In one way or another, each of our children had been bullied, rejected, and discriminated against. Each of us watched as they were unfairly denied experiences or opportunities that their brothers or sisters were privileged to enjoy. Each of us shared different stories of our children's paths to acceptance. I felt a strong friendship and mutual respect for everyone in the room— and it took a matter of minutes to feel that way. I was in a good place.

Our local PFLAG chapter was small and eventually folded because the previous leaders were moving on. I considered stepping up to keep the chapter alive, but I was already co-leader of the TransParent group at the Q Center. Although the number of PFLAG meetings we attended was probably less than a dozen, the friendships, resources, and opportunities gained were instrumental on our journey. Vince and I proudly marched in our first PRIDE

Parade with other members of PFLAG and we were honored to help carry the PFLAG banner.

PFLAG introduced us to a dear friend who is now like a second mother to my son. In fact, Drew actually calls her mom. While I might otherwise feel hurt at the thought of my son calling somebody else Mom, she has shown him all the kindness, compassion, acceptance, and support of a mom and has treated him like her own child.

PFLAG also connected us with another friend who referred us to the LGBT Resource Center at Syracuse University. There, we were invited to borrow a video, *Call me Kade*, which chronicled the life of a female to male transgender youth. I couldn't get there to pick up the video so I asked Vince to get it. Vince was very uncomfortable going someplace new and losing his anonymity. One of the challenges we had to overcome was the fear of the unknown, the social outcome, each time we outed ourselves as the parents of a transgender youth. Not yet ready to lose his anonymity, Vince did what I would expect. He searched the Internet until he found the video. It was older and very hard to find, but he did.

*Call Me Kade* was another turning point in our acceptance of Drew as our son. It chronicled the transformation of someone just like Drew—a transgender boy of similar age and circumstances. Suddenly most of the scariness of not knowing what was happening to Drew or that life was somehow ruined melted away. Kade and his family had put themselves out into the public so others like me and my family could learn and grow.

## Philadelphia Trans Health Conference

Although Drew knew we were there for him, it was important to show, through our actions, that our entire family was in it with both feet. We didn't know everything he was experiencing and feeling, but we were committed to learning what we needed to learn so that we could best support him and advocate for him.

Four separate people recommended that we attend the Philadelphia Trans Health Conference (PTHC): the social worker at Golisano Children's Hospital, the program coordinator at the Q Center, and our new friends, Karen and Jason. Four people who had already made such a positive difference in our lives couldn't be wrong, so we made our reservations and told Drew to check out the workshops for teens. Vince and I signed up for every workshop for parents and allies, as well as several designed for educators—splitting duties when two were scheduled at the same time. Attending this conference as a family was a way to show Drew he was not alone on this journey of discovery.

I remember looking at all the workshop titles and descriptions and getting very excited. There was a workshop for everything: hormones, parenting perspectives, transitioning in school, topics of significance for female to male transition, name changes, binding, top surgery, legal issues, and so much more. There were workshops about topics that affected Drew and our family immediately, and workshops for issues that were way down the road.

It wasn't until I got to the conference that I realized how much more there was for us beyond the workshops. I knew that going there was the right thing to do and was important, but I had no idea how much so until I actually experienced it.

By the time we attended the conference in May of 2011, Drew had already been living as a male in our home for six months. These were six intense months with a lot of growth, learning, and progress on his transition. He had been wearing a binder and presenting as a male. We had the pronouns down and told all our family and friends about Drew and his transition. We had seen a pediatric endocrinologist and Drew started hormone therapy (testosterone.) We had done and learned so much, that by the time May rolled around, I think we developed the attitude that we knew it all and didn't need to go to the conference. The reality at the conference proved otherwise! We were just scratching the surface; we were just starting. Our experience at the conference was like drinking water from a fire hose.

### Finding Hope at PTHC

For three days, the conference focused on everything transgender. As much as we had been immersing ourselves in reading and learning all we could, we were limited by what was available in Central New York as far as doctors, therapists, and professionals who had experience working with transgender people and their families. In our community, the number of transgender people and parents who have children who transitioned is small.

Everything we could need was there for us at the conference. It had a smorgasbord of specialists. You want to talk to surgeons? There's a whole bunch of them. You want to talk to people who have already had surgery? You got it. Therapists. Educators. Lawyers. Parents. Children. Clergymen. We met all of these people and heard firsthand about their experiences. All of our questions were answered; this time not just from textbooks and research, but by sitting and talking to real people, face-to-face.

Despite me being an engineer, always seeking facts through research, I also seek insight. I need to see, feel, and have an experience. That's how I learn and that's how I ultimately make decisions. I don't let my intuition and gut guide me completely, but listening to people, looking someone in the eye, and hearing about their journey enables me to understand and envision what's right or wrong for me.

At the Q Center, I met a few other transgender people and their families, but at the conference I got to meet hundreds and see thousands. I met people of all ages, in all stages of transition, and at all stages of their life. There were people already transitioned for many years who were in their twenties and thirties, out of college, in loving relationships, married, or gainfully employed. Many were living what I consider happy, healthy lives, and I became filled with hope.

The PTHC's gift to me was priceless: I gained another robust picture of what the future could look like for my son. For fifteen years, I envisioned a future for my daughter. Those images were now lost to me and for a while I had nothing to replace them with. I didn't know what my child's future would look like. The people I met at the PTHC provided me a realistic, hopeful picture of the future that awaited my son.

## How TYFA has helped

My first PTHC conference was largely shaped by an organization called TYFA, which stands for Trans Youth Family Allies. TYFA's founding members are parents of transgender youth who came together first to support each other. They now support hundreds of families. TYFA empowers children and families by partnering with educators, service providers, and communities to develop supportive environments in which gender may be expressed and respected. TYFA envisions a society free of suicide and violence in which all children are respected and celebrated.

At the conference, TYFA offered several workshops and an opportunity to connect with other parents. Many of those parents had children who transitioned before kindergarten.

I will never forget the first TYFA workshop I attended: *Minimizing the Top Ten Fears of Raising a Transgender/Gender Variant Child.*

One of the first things the executive president of TYFA shared as she voiced her early fears was: "Who is going to love my child?" Tears filled my eyes immediately. She said something that I had felt, but was afraid to ever say out loud. My love for Drew is so big that I don't know how to express it in words. I know how much love, goodness, kindness, and wonderfulness is within him, and I had this same fear. I often thought to myself, *Who will love my child? He is so deserving of love. Who will love him the way he deserves to be loved?* I was crying, and we were only minutes into the program.

The workshop was lively. More than a hundred parents started to raise their hands and share their fears. Just like my first Families

Anonymous and PFLAG meetings, I felt an immediate sense of connection, knowing others in the room had similar fears, questions, and experiences. Although we were all at different stages of our personal journeys, I now had a larger community. I was not alone.

I saw myself six months earlier in some people; brand new to the transgender issue and just learning. Some, although managing to get to the conference, were still in a state of doubt, disbelief, or denial. I saw people where we were then—several months into the journey. I had a sense of already knowing, accepting, and understanding what it means to be transgender.

I also got to see parents who were years down the road where their child had already transitioned. I could see we had an enormous responsibility to help our son through hormones, surgeries, a name change, school accommodations, transitioning outside our home. These new friends offered advice to make things easier and avoid common mistakes.

None of these steps were simple or trivial, so the help of others who had been through them was tremendous. There was so much to consider and do. For example, the name change process alone involves many steps beyond getting it approved by a court. There's also getting a revised Social Security card, birth certificate, passport, driver's license, school documents, insurance, and medical documents. I took for granted all the places where a birth name exists.

After leaving the Philly conference, TYFA continued to provide another vital resource: its listserv, which is a community like the Q Center, but online. TYFA's listserv is an email list that connects hundreds of families with transgender youth. People on the listserv gave me hope that our family's transition wasn't always going to be so overwhelming. People were sharing how they stepped through the process. Whenever somebody meets challenges, there is compassionate support and practical help.

My local community of parents with transgender children may be small, with roughly twenty in our TransParent group, but the TYFA listserv connects me with hundreds of other parents across the country. TYFA's listserv is a community of allies and angels, created by allies and angels.

### Developed Sense of Urgency from PTHC

The Philly conference filled me with an incredible sense of urgency. Drew was still a child (although he might argue with us about this). He was still growing. He was fragile. He was learning. It became apparent to me that there was still a lot of his childhood left. At age fifteen, he had two years left in high school; it was not too late for him to create childhood memories that he could look back on happily.

We met so many people at the conference who transitioned in their thirties, forties, or fifties. They lived their childhood and young adult years in the wrong bodies. They didn't get the chance to experience their childhood as their identified gender. We had the power to help Drew experience his remaining years of high school as a male.

I felt a need to get beyond the fact that he's transgender and get the focus back on how he's just a really great teenager. He's transgender, so what? Now, let's get on with the rest of life.

It became clear that I had a role to play in this transition. Initially, our approach was that of typical parents: cautious. "Alright, let's wait and see. If after you're eighteen you want to have surgery, if you're sure you want to do this, well then, we'll talk about it."

Going to the conference helped me understand that my role in Drew's time-sensitive transition was crucial. I could help my son experience at least part of his childhood as the boy he has always been. To do this; however, I realized the initial cautious approach wasn't going to work. Through the PTHC, I also learned waiting until Drew was eighteen wasn't necessary either. At this point we all knew, without any doubt, that Drew was a boy. Why put this arbitrary line in the sand that he can't start living and being who he really is until he is eighteen? Why deny him two years or more of being comfortable in his own skin? Why deny him the ability to create memories that he can look back on and feel good about?

---

### A Special Thanks to Chaz Bono

Chaz Bono spoke at the PTHC. I bought his book at the conference and read it before the trip was over. Reading his book and hearing his story contributed significantly to one of my major take aways from the conference—that there was still a chance for Drew to experience the latter part of his childhood as a boy.

What Chaz Bono represented to me, and one of the reasons I'm so grateful to him for sharing his story, is that he explains so well about the loss he experienced. He, as a transgender person, never had the childhood of a boy. Some of us are old enough to remember images of the little girl, "Chastity" on the Sonny and Cher show. Those images are not how Chaz sees himself. He created such a vivid, visible example of the years he lost; years that I have the ability to help Drew keep.

My heart breaks that Chaz doesn't have any period of memories growing up, even into his thirties, of being who he really is. He shares in his book, *Transition*:

> *Along with going through all of the changes that have happened as a result of transitioning, I have also experienced a deep sense of loss and profound sadness for the 40 years of life I spent inside of the wrong body. In addition to the elation that I have felt while becoming the man I was always meant to be, I have had to grieve that my life is half over and I am only now feeling like a complete human being. I grieve for my lost youth, for the boy and young man that I didn't get to be, and I grieve because I will never experience what it's like to grow up as a man, only what it's like to grow old as one.*
>
> *In spite of this sense of loss, which has now diminished greatly, I am more grateful than words can express for my life, and am happier and more fulfilled than I've ever been.*

I so admire Chaz for his courage to share his story publicly. He speaks so honestly about his feelings. He wants to increase awareness and help other kids have the opportunity to experience their childhood wholly, as themselves. He was brave to begin his gender transition in the public eye. By doing so, he continues to impact change and create awareness and visibility for the transgender community. As somebody who has been changed by it, I am forever grateful. His brave and unselfish actions have contributed to my awareness as a parent—helping me more quickly provide what my child needs.

Chaz helped me realize that I play a paramount role in driving Drew's transition. I don't know how long it would have taken for me to come to these realizations on my own. As well-intentioned as I am and as much as I love Drew, as much as I read every book I could get my hands on, as much as I researched every website I could find and talked to every doctor and professional I could; without meeting other people like Chaz Bono who are willing to be vulnerable and expose themselves in front of the whole world—knowing that a very large number of people are going to be critical and judgmental and mean—it could have taken me years. It's because of those stories and those people and the opportunity to meet them that I got to this place of acceptance and urgency as soon as I did.

Every day my respect grows ever stronger for those who can be so open about such personal topics, because it is so scary, so vulnerable, and so hard. It's kind of like pinning your heart on a bull's eye where people can take aim and shoot. You don't know how your story is going to be received—with empathy or with arrows. It can hurt, and yet, they do it anyway.

I recall standing in line at the conference, waiting to get my book signed by Chaz. As I watched him autograph books and take pictures, his kindness, compassion, and beautiful soul shined through. Many months later, I would hear from a mom on the TYFA listserv about how Chaz showed up at her door and surprised her young son with a visit. Chaz is a member of the Board of Transforming Families, a support group for families with gender diverse children. He's just a good person using his experience to help make a difference. I want to be like that.

# Chapter 10

# Becoming Andrew

*I watched Anderson last night and all I can say is "WOW"!*
*Drew is a completely different person! It was wonderful to*
*see him happy and talkative. I couldn't believe the difference.*
*I am so happy for him.*
—*School Counselor*

Even the most supportive and loving of parents can screw up.

Drew was having a bad week, enduring a period of significant dysphoria, which for him leads to increased anxiety and a desire to isolate from others. Dysphoria is characteristic of transgender people. They often feel very upset or depressed about the body they were born with. It can consume their mind because their gender is something they have to deal with every second of every day. This is very serious and very real. My son hates his body and at times those feelings are overwhelming. Gender isn't easily changed and it takes a lot of time and money to bring about the necessary changes.

Drew had been home from school for two days. As a seventeen-year-old transgender male trying to invisibly get through his senior year of high school, his anxiety was constant. From the moment he got on the school bus until he returned home, his anxiety did not let up. Some days; however, were worse than others and he couldn't go to school. We were on day two of such a period. We had gone on a college visit the previous Friday and it stirred up many emotions and fears in him, triggering this heightened dysphoria.

I started having the all-too-familiar mom experience. I saw my son struggling and I wanted to fix it for him. I wanted to hold him close and remind him how loved and wonderful and special he is. I wanted to take away his pain and worries and make it all better, at least for a little while.

So, from a heartfelt, well-intentioned place, I came up with what I thought was a brilliant idea. I decided to hold a special, spur-of-the-moment tree decorating party to take Drew's mind off his worries.

For years, even before we were married, Vince and I have always collected Christmas ornaments from places we've travelled and significant events we've shared. Each year, the decorating of our tree has been (in my experience) a joyful celebration and reminder of all we have, all we've done, and how much we have to be grateful for. Twenty-five years of ornaments provide a wonderful trip down Memory Lane of fun experiences that might otherwise have been forgotten.

The joyful tradition of decorating our tree included eggnog in fancy glasses, cheese and crackers, and holiday cookies coupled with laughter and stories as we reminisced.

This was the first time we decorated the Christmas tree together since Drew's transition. As I write this, I'm shaking my head and kicking myself for what I should have realized before my idiotic notion that a trip down Memory Lane would somehow cheer up Drew. What was I thinking?

Let's just say that decorating the tree together did not turn out to be the ideal Norman Rockwell scene I had envisioned—a picture of my family joyously laughing together as we recalled happy family times from the past—forgetting all our worries of today. The problem? All the Christmas ornaments associated with Drew throughout his childhood.

Drew had long since purged our walls of his childhood pictures. We had forgotten, however, that several ornaments bore his photo—a picture of a young girl he didn't identify with. A young girl that looked happy to me—always wearing a great big smile. What he saw; however, was somebody dressed as a girl who was already questioning who he was on the inside, but who didn't have the words to explain this confusion or share his feelings. Some of the photos are also painful reminders of the years he struggled alone and endured teasing and bullying.

Then there were all the ornaments with his birth name. Some were his precious, artistic creations from elementary school; others were vacation and holiday ornaments we had personalized with our names. Drew, like many transgender youth, did not like seeing, using, or being reminded of his birth name.

The pile of ornaments that would not go on the tree was getting bigger. It was a pile of fifteen years' worth of ornaments containing his birth name or photo. And Drew, who always puts others before himself, was trying to hide his feelings so that he wouldn't spoil the experience for us. Fortunately, he's a terrible liar.

When we were done, it appeared as if Billy was an only child. There was no trace of Drew's childhood on our tree of memories. Vince and I hope that one day reminders of his birth name will be taken in stride, but for now it is still a raw, painful memory. We went out and purchased two new family ornaments and had them personalized with Drew's name.

This happy family tradition clearly backfired. Instead of taking Drew's mind off the challenges of being a transgender teen, it shined a spotlight on them. Drew recovered quickly, just as he had when we were awkwardly learning to use his chosen name, as well as male pronouns. His compassion and patience with us during our learning curve set an example of who we want to be for him and others.

The tree decorating experience brought to mind painful new questions for me. As I realized that my experiences and my memories were not experienced in the same way by Drew, I began to question the memories in my mind, which were happy ones filled with laughter and smiles. Were they ever really happy for him, too? At what point did it become a struggle for him? At what point were the smiles in those photos not real or perhaps only temporary reprieves from the growing battle going on inside of him?

We know now that Drew struggled for a long time alone, hiding his pain from us. His lonely struggle almost cost him his life. As a mom, I would have given *anything* if I could have known sooner. Could I have lifted him out of that dark, lonely place sooner? Our beautiful son had our support from day one, but day one for us came only after he endured years of silent, overwhelming pain.

I'm eternally grateful for "day one"; we were granted the opportunity to support our son. The alternative is unthinkable. There is no group with a higher suicide rate than the transgender population, and transgender teens are the most vulnerable. Often, puberty can plunge them into a worsening nightmare of depression, anxiety, and suicidal ideation. Forty-one percent of transgender youth attempt suicide. Think about that … forty-one percent.

So we had a Christmas tree with a lot of empty branches this year, but I know those branches will one day be filled with new ornaments representing new happy memories. Being a family with a transgender child, transition has become a part of our life. We've learned how to transition through painful times and bounce back stronger and wiser than ever. Although at times the journey is difficult, we've learned that despite challenges and unsolved problems, we can do more than get by, we can thrive.

### Andrew is Official

The Christmas tree decorating incident emphasized that even with two years of transition behind us, we were still learning and adapting. Thankfully, we had a good start with many victories and positive experiences under our belt. Two years earlier, we took away one huge realization from Drew's stay at Golisano's Children's Hospital: how important it was to Drew that we use male pronouns and his preferred name.

We made sure that from day one his driver's license and permit identified him as Andrew Cook. His license indicates male and his ID reflects a handsome, happy teen. Now he has that photo with a genuine smile on his license to remember. It's really him in his memory; it's not somebody that he had to erase or hide or replace after he transitioned.

We had a sense of urgency to change Drew's name, because he was about to get a fresh start in eleventh grade at a new school. No problem ... or so we thought. Vince had learned how to do a legal name change at the Philly Trans Health Conference and through resources that we were connected with online. He drew up the necessary paperwork himself. After the three of us had our signatures notarized, Vince submitted the paperwork to the New York State Supreme Court office downtown. Who knew that you had to go to Supreme Court to change a name?

The self-prepared documents were OK, but the name change raised a red flag with the court. The judge was concerned about changing Drew's name from a clearly female name to a male one, even though our documents explained that he was transgender. The court assigned Drew a law guardian, which we had to pay for. The law guardian would determine whether the name change was in Drew's best interest and report back to the court.

The law guardian who was assigned didn't know anything about being transgender and certainly not about transgender youth. He was a good person, and we understood his predicament because we didn't know much about being transgender before Drew. While I hope and expect that people in certain positions like medical facilities, schools, or the courts would have appropriate knowledge of transgender issues, many people don't right now. That's one of the reasons why we wrote this book.

The people we were dealing with—the law guardian, judge, and other court officials—were all reasonable, open-minded, and compassionate, and we were very fortunate in that regard. I have no doubt that eventually the court would have granted our name change petition; however, timeliness was critical. If Drew's name was not legally changed before the start of the new school year, he would be listed on all school documents with a female name and gender marker. This introduced many risks, complications, disclosures, and accommodations that would have to be made at school—none of which would be necessary if his name was legally changed now.

If we didn't have to educate the court and prove that we were acting in Drew's best interest, we would have had plenty of time. This extra hurdle and expense put Drew's fresh start and transition in a new school in jeopardy.

In order to educate the law guardian and turn the name change around quickly, I reached out to all the professionals I knew—people who could help explain that this was not just a mom and dad on a crazy whim doing something harmful to their child. We wanted to prove that we had done our due diligence and had been supporting our son for years getting to this point. It wasn't a rash decision we were making. Furthermore, it was a change that was necessary and in Drew's best interest.

One of the first people to respond was Moonhawk River Stone, M.S., LMHC, a psychotherapist we met in Philadelphia. He called me as soon as he got my email. He jumped right in with, "How can I help? What's the situation?" He spent at least an hour on the phone in consultation with me, and then offered to do a conference call with the law guardian to answer his questions.

So, we did a teleconference with the law guardian, and Hawk was able to medically, scientifically, and professionally step through all the issues. Hawk was special because he was able to discuss the legalities of the name change for transgender people and cite legal cases in our state. In essence, Hawk was talking the language that the law guardian really knew. Hawk gave the law guardian information that would be effective in court because ultimately, it was the judge who needed to be convinced.

The Q Center's program coordinator, Heather, wrote a wonderful letter. She explained the concepts of gender identity, the gender spectrum, sexual identity, and how they differ and interrelate. She provided an excellent one-page education. She also knew Drew personally from youth groups at the Q Center and talked about what Drew was like when he first came to the Q Center. She had the experience of seeing him through the transition and how he has changed, how he has grown and who he is as a person.

Drew's therapist also had a significant impact on the name change. She had written a letter, but Vivian and the law guardian were having trouble connecting by phone. Always in Drew's corner, Vivian was persistent in her attempts to return the law guardian's phone calls. She finally reached him by phone while he was riding his bicycle to work the day of our court appearance. Vivian went above and beyond explaining how the name change was not just in Drew's best interest; it was imperative to his survival.

Vivian's comments complemented the education Heather had provided. She explained how gender and gender identity are not binary, but on a spectrum, and she explained where Drew fell on this spectrum. Some people can live their lives without a name change or other elements of transition. It's not easy, but some can put on one face for the world in order to keep their jobs and to keep their family. They can get through each day dressing and presenting as someone they're not. But Vivian explained to the law guardian that Drew was on the end of the spectrum where that wasn't going to work. Vivian's words resonated and the law guardian really understood.

Nearly a dozen others submitted letters on Drew's behalf: the endocrinologist, psychiatrist, school officials, and other specialists and professionals who worked with us over the years. Collectively, these letters and conversations connected the dots and provided the crash course of awareness, understanding, and acceptance, which had taken us years to accumulate.

It worked. The law guardian told Drew's story in court, wholeheartedly recommending that the judge grant the name change. His words brought many in the room to tears—tears of compassion upon hearing the story, and tears of joy upon seeing Drew's face when the judge granted the name change.

There was another reason to cry. Drew's day in court took place on his sixteenth birthday. When the judge was convinced the name change was appropriate, he not only recognized that it was Drew's birthday, but also that it was important to start school with his name corrected. The judge generously made arrangements with the law guardian and other court officials to bypass standard procedure and make the necessary changes to the court documents that day. Drew got his official name change on his birthday—what a nice present.

With Drew's name change now official, he was able to apply for his driver's license learner's permit using his male name. His paper trail as Andrew Cook had begun. Drew would never need to explain to future employers or college admissions staff why the name on his application does not match the name on file with previous employers, his high school diploma, or his college degree.

Drew went to school less than two weeks later with the correct name on the roster at his new school. Since then he has applied for college and jobs with an identity that matches who he is; there is no mismatched paper trail to explain. Progress may be slow, but our gratitude for the little things that most others take for granted is enormous.

### 'Coming Out' Can Be Hard for Parents, Too

The truth will set you free, but I can't always tell the whole truth. And that's a problem in my family right now. If you're reading this book, it's not a secret that we're the proud parents of an awesome young man who is transgender. But many of the people I know aren't aware that I have a transgender son. I've lost touch with many old friends, neighbors and colleagues, and to be honest, I've avoided running into them whenever possible.

Quite simply, it's hard and exhausting, and can be nerve-wracking because each time we share, we never know what the social outcome will be. In my experience, most people have been accepting, but not all. Most of my family, friends, neighbors, and work colleagues did not previously know a transgender person, so whenever I chose to share our experience I also ended up answering a lot of questions and doing a lot of educating. The time spent is well worth it when the result is a renewed friendship and the friend becomes one more ally in the world. However, sometimes the conversation doesn't have the same result and it ends abruptly in an awkward way.

Sometimes I think it would be easier to lose touch with a friend and not know whether they would be accepting and understand, than to find out that they're not. That feeling still comes up in me, despite the fact that I have had far more positive disclosure experiences than negative ones.

We've kept Drew's transition to ourselves for more reasons than the social outcome. I'm not simply worried about losing friends. If it was as simple as that, I would honestly rather know who will fully accept my son and who will not. If somebody is not going to accept Drew (or me for having supported his transition) then I don't want them in my life. We've been cautious about who we share with because of other real risks and dangers that exist, which I'll expand upon a bit later.

Whenever I run into an old friend or neighbor that I haven't seen in a few years, they naturally ask about my husband and family. Often they inquire about "my daughter" using his female birth name.

I've become a master of the elusive answer, which manages to disclose nothing while answering the question in an honest, but vague, way. *"Oh the kids are fine. We are all enjoying our new home"*

When somebody specifically asks about "my daughter," I make the decision whether it is somebody that needs to know and if this is the right time and place for a conversation, because disclosing means a conversation will follow. Explaining that the person they knew as my daughter is actually now my son and goes by a new name, well … that usually requires more of an explanation than can happen in the checkout line at the grocery store.

It's a constant battle, like a tug-of-war going on in my head. Do I tell or don't I? Is this person safe to disclose to or not?

Here lies a conflict we haven't fully resolved with Drew. I want to share this because I know it is a common dilemma experienced by many other families. Hopefully by sharing and shining a light on this, we can take steps toward increased awareness and changes in society that will make the issue and conflict irrelevant.

As far as Drew is concerned, being transgender is his private, personal business—it is *his* life— and it should be *his* decision, not ours, who to share it with. He should be the one to decide whether specific people get to know and whether that person's knowing poses a risk. He doesn't want to be "outed" to new friends and classmates unless and until *he* decides their friendship warrants telling them. People he doesn't have a relationship with don't need to know. Often, those are the people that pose a risk to Drew's safety and happiness, so he is careful about when and to whom he discloses.

I completely understand, respect, and embrace that, but it leaves us in a position that we still haven't reconciled. Vince and I know that Drew needs to be true to himself and live as his authentic male self, despite the challenges this poses in our society. That is why we fully supported his transition. At the same time, we need to be true to ourselves and live as *our* authentic selves. Our ability to do so is a challenge our family is still navigating.

Drew wants a fresh start, but we don't, entirely. There is a lot about our lives that we want to hang onto. Vince and I have forty-eight years of friendships—personal and professional relationships. There are hundreds, possibly thousands, of childhood friends, college friends, former neighbors, and professional colleagues that I have been avoiding for nearly two years so that I don't risk violating my son's wishes. That causes me so much pain and conflict because that is not authentically who I am. I need my friends, I value my personal and professional relationships, and I cannot hide something that is such an important part of my life and who I am. I don't feel any need to disclose to casual acquaintances, new people that I meet, or old friends who didn't even know I once thought I had a daughter. But to abruptly cut off or avoid forty-eight years' worth of old friends causes me a great deal of sadness.

Drew understands the importance of educating others and increasing awareness, and that is why he fully supports us writing this book and sharing our story. He also understands that publishing and publicizing our book increases the likelihood that old friends and neighbors will learn about his transition. At this time in his life; however, Drew chooses not to go on the book tour with us or share his photos, because he wants to move forward with a clean slate. We are sharing *our* story and simultaneously doing all we can to protect and respect his privacy. We are working together to manage those things we can control, while courageously dealing with those we can't.

No matter how widely available our book becomes, there will always be old friends, neighbors, and colleagues who we'll inevitably run into. We will eventually find a solution that works for our family regarding when, if, and how to appropriately handle disclosure in these situations. Drew has transitioned and our family has transitioned with him, but we're not finished yet. We are a work in progress—always growing, always changing, and navigating to a better place together.

I believe that I, and everybody in my family, will never be able to be who we were meant to be until we are totally free of this quandary; until it no longer controls how we live our lives and our day-to-day conversations, decisions, thoughts, and actions. In my opinion, to live my life authentically, being transgender (or having a transgender family member or loved one) needs to become normalized so no one feels the need to keep it a secret. It needs to become another understood and accepted element of human diversity. The stigma, fear, lack of awareness, and misinformation needs to be changed so that it becomes irrelevant.

Mixed race and mixed culture marriage had a stigma at one time, and so did being gay. Now, they are both widely accepted as a norm. I don't mean to marginalize any person's experience or say that it is one hundred percent better in every way or in every part of the world because I know that is not true. I have friends in mixed race marriages who have shared heartbreaking stories of discrimination and cruelty, and we are still fighting for marriage equality and equal rights for gay people in the United States. So as much as I wish it were otherwise, I know we are not "there" yet. Discrimination, ignorance, and intolerance are sadly still a reality. However, if you were to compare society and the media's response when Ellen DeGeneres came out in 1997 to where gay Americans are today, that's the kind of movement and shift in awareness and acceptance I hope to see with respect to being transgender.

The thing is, I don't see how that day will come if we hide, keep quiet, and wait for somebody else to make it better. I don't want to wait for somebody else to change the world and make it safe for me and my family to share that our son is transgender. Fundamentally, I don't think I have anything to hide; but due to societal stigmas, hiding continues, sending the message and perpetuating the stereotype that there is something wrong and it should be hidden.

So we are taking the risk, being vulnerable, and sharing our story. We have to be our authentic selves just as our son needs to be his authentic self. Hopefully in doing so, the truth will set more than the three of us free.

## The Beautiful Reality of Our Experience

When people learn of our family's experience, one of the first questions they ask is, "How did Vince handle this?" The next question is usually, "How did Drew's brother take the news?" When I'm asked that now, I can confidently respond that Billy loves his little brother, fully supports him, and has his back. However, that acceptance and understanding didn't happen overnight.

There are not enough resources available for helping siblings, and I hope the pool of resources will grow. I certainly could have used assistance with facilitating this disclosure. I struggled to find the best way to help 19-year-old Billy comprehend something that we were still figuring out ourselves.

When Drew transitioned, Billy was not living at home. Drew was the one to first tell him the news. It was Christmas Day in 2010, a little more than a month after Drew came out to me and Vince. Billy was spending the day at our house and the boys were up in Drew's room playing a video game. There was some small talk while they played, then Drew built up the courage to say, "So Bill, did you ever wish you had a little brother?"

According to Drew, Billy gave him a confused look and said, "No, not really." Then Drew said, "Well, you've got one." I don't know exactly how the conversation went after that. Drew may have tried to explain that he was really a boy in a girl's body. My sense is that Drew struggled to explain, but the conversation was strained. I can only imagine—it took me months before I was capable of confidently and effectively explaining this. Both of their anxiety levels went up and neither was really capable of adequately explaining or understanding or accepting.

Tension and discomfort remained between them for months. Billy didn't live at home, so they didn't see each other often; however, when Billy did visit, he frequently used female pronouns and Drew's birth name. I don't believe it was an intentional rejection. I know how hard it was for me to make the change, after 15 years of female pronouns and another name. I slipped up many times, but Drew patiently and lovingly corrected me. He knew my mistakes were genuinely mistakes and that I was trying. I believe it was difficult for Billy, and he didn't have the opportunity that we had to be around Drew all day, every day. When changing any habit or learning anything new, you need plenty of practice and application. We spent all our time with Drew, which provided ample opportunity to make our mistakes, correct them, and get lots of practice. The change took a lot longer for friends and relatives who didn't see us or Drew as often. It's understandable.

Drew felt that Billy didn't accept him, and he started to avoid him—hiding from the awkward encounters. Many weeks went by and the boys did not see each other. Whenever we went out and knew we'd be seeing Billy, Drew made other plans or came up with an excuse to stay home. When Billy came to visit, Drew wasn't home.

During this time, over a series of conversations, Vince and I explained to Billy that the person he thought was his sister was really his brother. Understandably, he was confused and had a lot of questions, which we tried our best to answer. It took time for

Billy to process this, but with each conversation we could see Billy soften as he started to express his concern for his brother.

We desperately wanted to bring our family back together again, so that we could all stop walking on eggshells. We needed to reintroduce our kids to each other and try again. Although Vince and I wanted to "rip off the Band-Aid" and get the introduction over with, we knew we had to follow Drew's lead.

One day Drew and I were out together, and I got a call from Billy on my cell phone. He needed some of his belongings, which were in the back of my car. We were only a few minutes from where Billy was staying and more than half an hour from our home. Although Drew wanted to be dropped off at home before I met with Billy, that would have required an hour of extra driving. Reluctantly, he agreed to go with me. I could see the anxiety building as Drew's entire body tensed, his leg pulsated up and down rapidly, and his breathing deepened.

When I pulled into the driveway, Billy walked out to meet us. I got out of the car and opened the hatchback to unload Billy's things. Drew sat quietly in the car, looking down and avoiding the possibility of eye contact with his brother. I struggled, searching for the best way to handle the situation. Do I force the issue and ask Drew to get out of the car to help unload? Was he ready for that? And what would Billy say and do? Did I make a terrible mistake bringing Drew here before he was ready to see his brother?

Billy, as he has often done, got us all through the awkward situation. Before I could say or do anything he said, "Hey, you've got Drew with you! Aren't you going to get out of the car so I can give my little brother a hug?"

I watched as weeks of tension, dread, and sadness were released from Drew's body. He got out of the car with a relieved smile on his face and hugged his big brother. The awkward meeting was now behind us. Without words, my sons communicated their love, loyalty, and acceptance through that beautiful hug. Although Billy still didn't fully understand, and worried about how his friends would react if they found out, he loved his little brother and had his back. From that point forward, Billy never messed up pronouns or Drew's new name. He understood how important this was to his brother.

Another example of our family's reaction can be found in the words written by my father in Drew's sixteenth birthday card:

> *To Drew, my grandson,*
>
> *I wish you love and happiness and success on your journey of life. Everyone in your family loves you so very much and supports you 100%. I pray for your peace every day and will always love you; after all you are my grandson.*
>
> *Love, Grandpa*

This sentiment captures the type of response we received from all our family members upon sharing that Drew was transitioning from female to male. We've been blessed. I know it doesn't go so well for all transgender individuals. That's partly why the rates for suicide, depression, and homelessness are so high.

Along with our family, we found most of our friends and work colleagues to be equally supportive. I have friends who have since become active and staunch allies, whereas they previously (like me) didn't know anybody transgender or what that even meant. I have been amazed how, in each sharing of our story, somebody will approach me later and share that either they or somebody close to them has a child, friend, neighbor, or other family member who could benefit from talking to me.

I was invited to share my story several times at work. I became very active in Lockheed Martin's Pride Employee Resource Group and spoke frequently throughout the organization. After making these small group presentations, many would approach me, grateful for my sharing. One man that I've known for years shared that he, too, has a transgender child who had recently transitioned from male to female. He did not feel he could share this with anybody at work until hearing my story. Another woman approached me and said she believed I was an angel placed in her path for a reason. She had a close friend whose child was struggling just as Drew had struggled years before. Her child and child's therapist tried to explain gender identity to her, but the mom felt alone and didn't know where to turn. She later introduced me to her friend and we spoke for hours.

Each time we share, the social outcome is usually better than we feared it might be. We educate a few more people in the world, and we often find ourselves connected to somebody with a similar experience who doesn't know where to turn to for help; just where we were a few short years ago. We're learning, one day at a time, to feel the fear and do it anyway. By facing my fears, I slowly, gradually overcome them, and can be my authentic self.

---

### Transgender in the Media

For the past two years, I have volunteered my time sharing our story and participating in training aimed at increasing awareness in different communities. At a workshop called, *Gender Identity and Youth: Supporting Parents*, I was asked to participate on a panel and share my experience as the parent of a transgender youth.

The workshop began as many do, with an icebreaker aimed at getting participants thinking and sharing in some way. On this day, the workshop facilitator posed the following question: "What do you remember from your first introduction to the transgender community?"

She paused and gave us time to reflect. I looked around the conference room. The tables were arranged in a "U" shape, so I could easily see the faces of the other attendees, which included educators, social workers, counselors, and service providers. The other participants seemed guarded; they looked nervous, curious and timid. The facilitator smiled patiently as we considered our responses.

My response should have come easily, as I was there not to learn, but rather to help teach. However, I found myself struggling to come up with an answer. My first introduction to the transgender community must have occurred sometime within the last few years, since Vince and I knew nothing about the transgender community until we had to learn, until our son's life depended on it.

Was it the day when I found Drew curled up on the floor, when he told me he would never fit in and never be accepted, and he needed to be someplace safe? Was it the day when I found my son covered in blood, so broken, frightened, and hopeless that he tried to end his own life? Was it the day my son shared, with tears in his eyes that he sometimes felt more like a boy than a girl? Was it the day we received the diagnosis of Gender Identity Disorder at the hospital? Was it the day our family travelled to Philadelphia to attend our first Trans-Health Conference, and met hundreds of transgender people and their families and loved ones?

Or was it that day seventeen years ago when my perfect, beautiful child was born? When the nurse placed him in my arms and exclaimed, "It's a girl!" Knowing what I know now, was that my first introduction?

I kept searching back through my memories trying to pinpoint the experience I would share when it was my turn to respond.

Then it hit me. My thoughts were flooded with memories of television talk shows from the eighties and nineties. Images filled my mind as if I had just seen the shows the day before. I remembered guests who were victims of violence or involved in the sex trade. They were sensationalistic, derogatory shows, which presented the transgender community in a negative light. The guests were portrayed as men who dressed as women intending to "fool" other men and play out deviant sexual perversions. The talk show hosts, according to my memory, appeared transphobic and antagonistic, ridiculing the guests and engaging the audience in mockery. The hosts were patronizing. Audience members booed and expressed their contempt for the guests. Some spewed angry comments as the host ran around the studio audience to capture their thoughts with the microphone.

I'm reminded of a Maya Angelou quote: "I've learned that people will forget what you said, people will forget what you did, but people will never forget how you made them feel."

I didn't remember the specific dialog from the talk shows or the specific guests, but what I remembered clearly was how the shows made me feel about transgender people and about how society would judge and respond to transgender people. The shows I remember led to misconception; there was a complete lack of understanding and empathy. I was made to feel that this lifestyle was a choice, an abhorrent choice. The guests were portrayed as sexual deviants, disgraceful, less than. And the audience was encouraged to participate in judgment, ridicule, and criticism.

I was never made to feel that these could be people who might have felt trapped in a body that doesn't belong to them. I was never led to feel compassion for their experience and struggle, but rather judgment for their choice of lifestyle. The shows made no distinction between sexuality and gender identity. I imagine some talk shows and hosts must have endeavored to bring gender identity and compassion into the discussion, but I don't recall any such shows. I don't remember ever feeling that the intent behind the talk shows was for empathy, education, or awareness; only sensationalism, exploitation, and shock value.

I remember only adult transwomen appearing on these shows; that is, people born with a male body but who identify and present as a woman. Never did I see a female to male transsexual on these talk shows, and I certainly never saw children.

As I shared my memories of these talk shows with the workshop participants, I was overcome with questions and filled with anger about the impact these shows had on me and my family. Hadn't we watched our son struggle for years, nearly losing all hope as we desperately searched for the source of his pain and unhappiness? It never occurred to me that he was struggling with a gender identity issue. Could that be because the little bit of awareness I did have was gleaned from sensationalistic talk shows that never actually educated me about gender and sexuality? What I saw my son experience was in no way portrayed on these talk shows. If these shows educated rather than sensationalized, would I have recognized sooner the source of my son's struggles?

How much of what I felt after watching those shows contributed to my limiting beliefs and fears, for me and my son? I was plagued with fears of judgment, rejection, and violence from the community if our "secret" was ever exposed. I remember how the shows made me feel about society's perception of transgender people. The audience was united in their rejection, reaction, and condemnation of the guests. Suddenly I understood where this subconscious fear I had carried for so long originated. I had watched and felt the disdain of talk show hosts and their audience members. Surely society would judge me and my son the way they had judged those brave talk show guests.

After the workshop, the memories of these shows and the feelings they stirred continued to haunt me. It led me to scour the

Internet for some of the old footage. What I found reinforced the general feelings I recalled from decades earlier.

I found an episode of the Phil Donahue Show that came to my mind the day of the workshop. For the most part, my memories were accurate. Watching more closely, I did see attempts by the host to present a balanced perspective. He was not as hostile to his guests as I recalled, although several audience members were. I would in no way give rave reviews for his coverage of the topic, treatment of his guests, or handling of the audience; however, a broader review of talk shows from that era showed he was not the worst perpetrator promoting misinformation, judgment, and intolerance.

Midway through the episode, as the hostile, judgmental voices of his audience grew louder, Phil Donahue said, "If we're not proud of this, maybe we don't understand it."

So true. So very true. If only the direction of the show, and others like it, changed at that point to help move the audience and home viewers toward understanding. Perhaps then I might have stored in my subconscious just a bit of awareness that would have helped me sooner to understand my own child's inner struggle, confusion, and pain.

Thankfully, much progress has been made in recent years.

### Anderson Cooper

In October 2011, TYFA was contacted by producers of Anderson Cooper's new morning talk show, *Anderson*. They were doing a show entitled, *Children & Teens Trapped in the Wrong Bodies*.

The show was an opportunity to increase awareness about transgender youth, educate parents about how they can support their children, and demonstrate the difference it can make in a child's life to be able to live as their true selves. Experienced professionals were lined up as guests, and TYFA was asked for help in finding families willing to share their story.

It is my wish to help other families and change the system to make it easier and more acceptable for those who follow in our footsteps. I responded and expressed an interest since the call was for parents, not youth. Drew was now two months into eleventh grade at a new school. He was "stealth" and happy and I didn't even consider asking him to be on the show. However, I did spend considerable time discussing how he felt about me being on the show. He gave a thumbs up with no hesitation. Only first names were to be used and there would be no mention of where we lived. None of Drew's new friends knew what I looked like or watched *Anderson*, so he wasn't the least bit worried. He told me to go for it!

Although I was actively sharing our story in our community and at my workplace, until then it had never occurred to me to go on national television.

I responded and agreed to speak with the producers. I was cautious because I did not want to be part of an exploitive or sensationalistic show. I watched Anderson Cooper for years on CNN and other news programs. I checked out the format and tone of his new talk show. I trusted him and was optimistic he'd present a respectful, informative show; still, "trust, but verify" was my approach.

My first phone call with the producer was more about me asking her questions rather than the other way around. Would I be talking to Anderson or answering questions from the audience? Who were the other guests and experts? Were they all positive and respected, or controversial? I did not want to be ambushed by negative or critical guests, or audience members spewing hate or inciting arguments. I wanted to be part of a show that would educate, increase awareness, instill compassion, and open minds.

The producers were as professional as I'd expect to be working with Anderson Cooper. After our second or third phone call, they asked if they could speak with Drew to get more of his experience in his own words. They felt his story and his spirit were compelling and asked how he would feel about participating from the audience. It was clear Drew wanted to help other teens like him, just as he had been helped by others who shared their stories and transition online. After additional phone interviews, we were asked how we'd feel about appearing onstage with Anderson.

Drew was tentative, so we were about to back out. This was something we had to be "all in" for—no doubts or hesitation. On another phone call, the producer disclosed they had several male-to-female youth (and their parents) on the show, but Drew was the only female-to-male. I quickly contacted Tyler, the new program coordinator at the Q Center, and recent college graduate. He is a dynamic, well-spoken, and simply remarkable person who also happens to be a transgender male. He was comfortable, actually excited, to have me provide his name and number to the producers. As I expected, after one phone call, they fell in love with Tyler, and he and his mom were booked as guests.

The producers asked if Drew would want to appear on stage with Anderson along with me, Tyler and Tyler's mom. The idea of being on the couch with Tyler made Drew instantly comfortable and he enthusiastically agreed.

The experience was a very positive one! Drew had come so far over the past year. The prep we did to determine whether he was truly ready for national television made that crystal clear! We didn't take it lightly; we put a lot of time and thought into being on the show, and Drew completely convinced us that he *wanted* and was ready to do the show. This was a huge step in his growth, development, and movement beyond the struggles he had over the previous years. Drew knew it was possible that he would be "outed" and his new friends may find out about the show. He was ready for that if it happened, but it didn't.

We were clear on our boundaries, and the producers respected our wishes. Among other things, we insisted on not disclosing Drew's birth name. Although the other youth did disclose their birth names, Drew did not want his used, and the producers did not push us.

I was so impressed by how compassionate the producers were and equally impressed with Anderson Cooper. They clearly did their homework before speaking with us. I found the producers to be more knowledgeable of transgender youth than many of the doctors, educators, and professionals I had dealt with over the years.

What was even more touching was their genuine interest in Drew's well-being. They knew Drew had previously attempted suicide. Although this was important to share, to help viewers understand how deeply this affects people, they were worried about the effect being on the show might have on Drew. They knew how far he had come and did not want to contribute to a backslide. Anderson Cooper is extremely sensitive about the topic, having lost his brother to suicide years earlier. He insisted that senior producers talk to both me and Drew. He needed to be certain we were confident there was no risk to Drew.

We were well ahead of him, having already discussed this with Drew and his therapist ad nauseum. As a mom, that's a risk I would not have taken. Collectively, we all agreed that this was a very positive step that was helping Drew—turning something so difficult and painful in his life into something good. He was now able to use his past to help others like him. I so appreciate the extra mile that the producers and Anderson took to put my son's well-being above their show and ratings. In the end, it was that kind of commitment and ethic that resulted in such a positive, informative, compassionate, well-done show. I am proud we were a part of it.

Anderson is a great guy. Sitting on the couch speaking with him, I felt like I was talking to an old friend. He took time to meet with all the kids and families. After the show he came back to the green room and took pictures with us. He had another episode to film that day, but he took time and treated each of us as important and valued guests. It was an experience I'll never forget.

## A Groundbreaking Shift

Much has changed since the talk shows of the eighties and nineties. Since the Anderson Cooper episode aired, I have seen Katie Couric, Jeff Probst, and Ricki Lake present equally positive shows on the topic of transgender youth.

The groundbreaking media shift began in 2007 when six-year-old Jazz and her family courageously shared their story with Barbara Walters on *20/20*. Jazz has continued in the media with the documentary, *I am Jazz*, which aired on OWN in 2011, a *20/20* update in 2013, and numerous other television appearances. I met Jazz and her mom, Jeanette, on several occasions and have so much respect and appreciation for all they continue to do to raise awareness and support transgender youth and their families. Dozens of parents on the TYFA listserv have shared how the *20/20* episode with Jazz saved their child's life by helping them to understand, and then providing them with something they could share with family and friends to explain what was happening with their own child.

The courage that Jazz and her family have shown is beyond my comprehension. Jazz is an unusually confident child who wanted to disclose long before appearing on television. She has always been comfortable talking about it and never wanted her parents to take down pictures of her when she appeared to be a little boy. Disclosing means educating, which in turn, produces lots of good. I'm thankful for the courage that Jazz and her family have shown. I hope one day I can impact lives in the same way they have.

**Chapter 11**

# Supporting the Physical Transition

*If you judge people, you have no time to love them.*
*—Mother Teresa*

Vince and I eventually reached a place where we knew without a doubt that Drew was a male trapped in a female body. We knew he had to live as his authentic self, and that required changes medically and socially. Some of those changes are reversible, some are not. Each has risks and dangers. Unfortunately, there is no easy answer or "one size fits all" solution. Transition for a transgender person is not fool proof, nor is it risk free.

Drew's dysphoria was significant. We were looking for ways to best support him—in some ways to keep him alive—until the magic age of eighteen when we could evaluate surgical options. Gender dysphoria worsens significantly at puberty. You cannot just will dysphoria away by being a parent who encourages an own-body-accepting attitude.

At age fifteen, Drew took matters into his own hands, first asking us to call him by his chosen name, Andrew, and to use male pronouns. It was the beginning of his social transition, which began at home and quickly progressed outside our family. We nicknamed him Drew, which he accepted, and the moniker has stuck ever since.

Drew needed physical transition, too. Within weeks of letting us know he was trans, Drew was using a common makeshift binding technique with Ace bandages to hide his chest. After a while, the bandages had served their initial purpose, but Drew realized he needed a real binder. He quietly came to me and explained that a binder was a special undergarment trans people wear to hide their chest. He needed our help to purchase one, which we did. I'm grateful he came to us because the type of binding he was doing with Ace bandages is dangerous and painful. Ace bandages constrict far more than is safe and can lead to fractured ribs and breathing problems.

A binder is safer than Ace bandages, but still torturous, and a person wouldn't wear one for fun. Drew wore his all the time. On a three-day trip staying in a single hotel room, Vince and I couldn't help but see how hard it was for him. It was hard for him to breath. It hurt. It was terribly hot. But he wouldn't be caught anywhere without it.

It is cruel irony that trans men wear a binder to be comfortable. There is nothing comfortable about a binder, yet the physical discomfort is nothing compared to the emotional discomfort of being anywhere in public without it.

Drew wore the binder for months, from morning to night. We gained confidence that he was not only transgender, but also suffering from severe dysphoria.

**Time for T**

Up until this point, everything about Drew's transition had been reversible: a short haircut, a new masculine wardrobe, male name and pronouns, and wearing a binder. About six months after his initial transition, Drew started asking about hormone therapy, specifically testosterone (or "T" for short). Fortunately, staff at the Q Center had expertise in this area and directed us to a pediatric endocrinologist who worked with transgender youth and was very good with teens. With the recommendation of Drew's therapist, and a thorough review of his documented history, the doctor began a very conservative course of hormone therapy (periodic T injections).

The endocrinologist does not just blindly administer cross-sex hormones. There are clinical guidelines indicating treatment following a diagnosis of gender dysphoria, psychotherapy or counseling, and a "real-life experience" in which the person lives full-time in the desired gender before beginning irreversible physical treatment.

We were required to sign an informed consent for testosterone therapy, which clearly spelled out all the risks and changes, both permanent and reversible, which may occur as a result of using testosterone. We approached this decision as seriously and diligently as everything else on this journey.

As many people know, testosterone causes hair growth, changes to body fat distribution, and voice deepening. Drew went through his second puberty, this time a male puberty, over the course of

several months. He made hilarious videos documenting his progress, some of which appeared on the Anderson Cooper show.

The purpose of Drew's videos was to share the process and
progress of his transition with other trans men around the world.
Similar videos were a lifeline and a source of hope for Drew in the
year before his transition. He was now doing the same for others.

Seeing Drew every day, it is easy to miss the subtle changes
that occur over time. Watching a video he made months earlier,
the dramatic changes become much more apparent.

We refer to Drew's videos as hilarious because in them he jokes
about things such as hair growth in odd places—like his knuckles!
What's up with that? What is wonderful is that these videos document more than his physical transformation, they document the
sparkle returning to our son's eyes. His smiles, laughter and humor
had returned. The child we lost years ago was back, and it was all
captured on these videos.

Testosterone did what all of the anti-depressants and anti-anx-
iety medications could not. It permanently alleviated some of the
wrong-gendered features contributing to Drew's dysphoria. We
had taken a big step forward while still only sustaining a mild risk
of permanent consequences in the unlikely event we were wrong.
Stopping testosterone would possibly leave some permanent un-
wanted hair and a deeper voice.

Some will undoubtedly criticize us as parents for allowing our
child to take a cross-sex hormone. I would ask those individuals to
consider that prior to testosterone, Drew was prescribed five different medications, which he had to take daily in order to manage his

depression, anxiety, ADD, and the side effects brought on by the other medications. Drew has since been weaned off all but one of those prescriptions. His overall health and well-being since being on T is better than it ever was. We often joke that T is the best anti-depressant around. Yes, there are potential risks, but none as dangerous to his health as trying to survive life in the wrong gender.

There was never a moment when we considered stopping T or thought it might be a mistake. Drew has made remarkable progress in his therapy. There were major psychological and social improvements as he has transitioned into a more confident, social, outgoing, and happy young man.

Testosterone brought about a significant change in our son, and each day restores the child we almost lost. We were warned of mood swings, aggressive behavior, and personality changes that come with a second puberty, but honestly we saw little of this. Drew is so much happier and engaged in life, that the positive changes have offset or masked any negative side effects.

### Surgery, at fifteen?

Drew started testosterone less than two weeks before the Philly Trans-Health Conference. At the time, we thought we had at least two or three years before considering the next logical step in Drew's physical transition: top surgery. However, as we shared in the previous chapter, the PTHC developed our sense of urgency, and our understanding that we were the ones who had drawn and reinforced the arbitrary line in the sand of age eighteen.

This change of heart and realization was most profoundly seen in Vince. He had joined Drew in the hotel gym for a workout and observed how difficult it was for him to breath and move with the binder. Since Drew had transitioned, he began working out daily at a local YMCA. Suddenly, Vince could visualize our son struggling through his daily workouts, yet committed and determined to do them in order to develop his new male body. He witnessed the struggle and understood that this was Drew's daily reality.

It was a very warm weekend in Philly and in sharing a small hotel room, we couldn't help but see how hot and uncomfortable Drew was. He developed a rash, which was getting steadily worse, but nothing could convince him to take a break from the binder.

Wearing a binder was not a long-term solution. We get that it's a necessity for most trans men to bind, but it's not something that should be done for an extended time. Before the conference, we thought it would suffice until Drew turned eighteen. During the conference, we came to understand it has too many negative health impacts that would make normal life impossible if he had to wait two or more years. Later, after surgery, we saw joyous activities like swimming and sports return that reinforced the decision.

The issue of top surgery was particularly relevant at the conference. Just saying the words "top surgery" before attending the conference was hard for Vince. They were hard for him to say even in private. Being immersed in the conference made the concept an easier part of normal conversation. Let's say we never went to the conference. If Vince had to call up a doctor and ask to schedule top surgery for our fifteen-year-old, I think that would have been an impossible social hurdle for him to overcome. It wouldn't have happened. The conference gave him that confidence. It gave him trust that doctors would know what he was talking about and that it was necessary and important.

Vince became involved and committed. Whereas he couldn't even say "top surgery" before the conference, he immediately took action to schedule Drew's surgery upon returning home. We began accumulating the appropriate referrals and documentation necessary to move forward.

Drew was over the moon! This was beyond his wildest dreams. You see and hear of so many young people who believe they are entitled, expect to be given whatever they want, and take things for granted. Drew is nothing like that. He is the most grateful person who knows how fortunate he is, and he never misses an opportunity to express his appreciation.

Top surgery was necessary because breast development that took place during his first (female) puberty couldn't be reversed with hormone treatment. Technically, top surgery for Drew was a double mastectomy with nipple reconstruction. Throughout the decision process and the procedure itself, Drew had been involved in all aspects from selecting the procedure and doctor, to assessing the risks, and even helping pay for the procedure. He has followed medical advice and treatments explicitly.

Of course, we are exposed to potentially greater risk with top surgery in the unlikely event that we are wrong and Drew changes his mind about transitioning. However, the procedure is cosmetically reversible with another surgery. Our feeling going forward about risk is that it would be a far greater risk to ignore our son and the challenges he's facing. If you are blessed with a transgender child, you will also discover that being transgender is not at all a choice for them. Suppressing and rejecting a transgender child robs them of their childhood and adds tremendously to the burden of transition later in life.

In an earlier chapter, I shared how Drew's childhood photos could now reflect a sequential storyboard. If I could share photos of Drew over the years from being a happy child to a depressed child, a withdrawn teen to the engaged, joyful young man he is today, you couldn't help but feel our emotional experience as parents. Similarly, the photo taken of Drew the morning after his top surgery, when the doctor first removed his bandages and replaced the dressings—that photo is priceless. The smile on his face lit up the room. The expression in his eyes is a combination of joy, disbelief, and overwhelming gratitude. If the day comes when he chooses to write his own memoir, I have a collection of beautiful photos to complement it.

Since the surgery, our son has emerged as a shirtless wonder! For years, he hid beneath a binder, baggy T-shirts and oversized hoodies. In the heat of summer, he would still hide beneath those layers. Now, he proudly (and constantly) walks around without a shirt, even in the middle of winter. As a child, Drew loved to swim. Our new home, which we moved into two years earlier, has a beautiful pool. Drew had not been swimming for more than four years and swore up and down that he didn't care and didn't like swimming anymore. Since his top surgery, he has returned to the pool. It wasn't swimming that he didn't like, just the body in the swimsuit.

In 2011, our employer did not offer transgender-inclusive benefits, so we had no insurance coverage for Drew's top surgery. While this presented a financial hardship and significant expense we hadn't planned for, we knew it was necessary. Not being bound by an insurance company's rules did, however, allow us to research and select the surgeon we believed was best qualified to perform our son's surgery. We selected a surgeon out of state, so we had to incur travel expenses and an extended hotel stay, as well as out of pocket payment in advance for the surgery. The results were perfect and there were no complications, so the surgeon we selected was worth the expense.

Top surgery is an expense and a hardship that many trans individuals spend years saving for. Although we wished our employer's insurance policy covered the surgery, we were grateful to have good jobs that provided the extra money necessary so we could pay for it ourselves. We borrowed against our 401K savings, a decision we don't regret. As a side note, in 2012 Lockheed Martin updated its policy to be transgender-inclusive and cover gender reassignment surgery, such as top surgery. Knowing what we know now—seeing the impact that top surgery has had on Drew—I often wonder if we would have waited the six months for the coverage had we known it would be offered. Perhaps we would have, but we'll never know.

---

### Transgender Awareness Among Physicians

It was quite surprising to hear that my primary care physician knew nothing about being transgender or treating a transgender patient. I was sitting in his examination room for my own exam when he asked how "my daughter" was doing. I explained and began his education. After a few minutes, he called in one of his nurses and a medical student so they could learn, too. I'm grateful they were open-minded and wanted to learn. I'm sad because I had to be their teacher. At my next appointment, I dropped off a couple of peer-reviewed articles, which I hoped he would read and share.

My primary care physician also happened to be Drew's. I'm grateful Drew wasn't with me when I learned our doctor didn't know much about his condition. As hard as it is for me to always be the educator and advocate for my son, instead of just his mom, it is harder for Drew. Although the doctor, nurse, and medical student were respectful when asking their questions, Drew doesn't like being anybody's case study. I think it brings him back to the bullying days when kids told him he was a freak. Having to explain himself to people in the medical community could reinforce his previous belief that those bullies were right.

I later learned of another physician in the practice that did have experience treating transgender patients. I switched Drew over to his care.

A year later, Vince and I were talking to a young doctor just out of a prestigious medical school. He was a friend who had known our family for years. We hadn't seen each other in a while. When he asked how "our daughter" was doing, we explained that our son Drew was doing very well and had transitioned from female to male the previous year. He too, like my primary care physician, had no idea about transgender people or gender dysphoria. Recently out of med school and starting his residency, we assumed he would have been educated in this area. We were surprised, to say the least, that he had no idea.

Last fall, Vince and I were at a writer's conference having a casual conversation with a doctor sitting next to us. He candidly admitted he had heard of transgender, but he added, "I get gays and lesbians, but I don't understand transgender." Ouch.

I expected doctors to know about transgender individuals, at least to some degree. For instance, most doctors learn about dextrocardia, a condition where the heart is on the right side of the chest. Dextrocardia is rare. A doctor wouldn't necessarily be a specialist or an expert who could diagnose or treat dextrocardia, but I think they would have enough awareness to recognize a potential problem and refer a patient to an appropriate specialist for the diagnosis and treatment. I have since adjusted my expectations.

Perhaps my expectation that a doctor should know everything is unfair. I'm sure not all medical schools teach about gender dysphoria and transgender issues. For those medical schools that do have training, perhaps it's optional.

I sometimes worry how much awareness training and media coverage will be necessary to get the general public up to speed and normalize being transgender in our society, if doctors coming out of medical school aren't even aware.

Subsequent visits to our primary care physician were impressive. We had to advocate for our son, educate some of the staff, and express our wishes, but they responded and were very respectful. The staff was nearly perfect in their use of male pronouns and Drew's chosen name. Prior to Drew's legal name change, he would sit in a waiting room fearful that the nurse would call out his female birth name, but they never did. We had similar positive, experiences at the offices of our dentist, Drew's therapist, and his psychiatrist.

This isn't the experience of every transgender person, unfortunately. Although there are plenty of just plain mean people, I believe the confidence and support we gave and still give Drew helps the situation tremendously. Other adults tend to respect the direction and choice parents make to support their child, even if they don't agree.

Many children's hospitals now have teams dedicated to supporting transgender youth, which is a sure sign of positive change. Jazz and her mom, who I introduced in the last chapter, participate in training at medical schools. Awareness is growing, and although it is not perfect, things are certainly moving in the right direction.

**Chapter 12**

# Engaging a New Life

*When we are no longer able to change a situation, we are challenged to change ourselves.*
*—Viktor E. Frankl*

By the end of the summer before eleventh grade, Drew would have the bulk of his transition from female to male complete, but it was still very new. There weren't many slip ups with pronouns or pouting the loss of our daughter. We were comfortable at home with Drew as our son. Our families and all of Drew's close friends were onboard and supportive. In fact, nobody Drew came out to expressed any genuine concerns.

While Drew was still a sophomore, we stressed about his junior year. We were worried about anxiety and bullying if Drew went back to the same school. We again hired the educational consulting firm we used for Billy to help assess our options. They had been fantastically supportive when we were seeking appropriate rehab facilities and educational programs for Billy.

Drew was already comfortable with our educational consultant, Betsy. They met and had talked previously. We met again now as a group to see what our options were for eleventh grade.

Betsy investigated alternative high schools and boarding schools within driving distance and finally suggested two in Vermont that we should visit. One would turn out to be really nice, but a little too therapeutic like the schools Billy attended. The other school, Rock Point, was perfect. We told the staff about Drew's situation, and they were very accommodating and convincing. What's even better, Drew liked the people and the program. He wanted to go.

Rock Point was in our back pocket all spring. We pictured Drew thriving there, and he might not be alone—there was possibly another trans kid already enrolled. To top it off, Rock Point had an excellent educational program, and Drew seemed to want to reengage in learning.

By summer; however, Drew would be vested in his growing cadre of close Q Center friends and relied on them for reinforcement. I don't know if it was the thought of leaving them or the fact that he had them for support, but Drew decided he wanted to stay close to home.

When we were looking at boarding schools, Betsy had also told us about an alternate public high school in a neighboring county. The owner of the consulting firm worked with the school through his position at a local university. He knew firsthand how the alternate school's program was designed to benefit at risk children like Drew. He said he thought a second school was cloned in our area.

We wanted Drew to go to Rock Point, but we had learned the hard way several times that it usually did not work out well if we forced our way. However, we were still skeptical Drew could make it through the year at the public school because he ended up homebound the previous three years. We did some digging and the consultant was right. Another alternative high school did exist in our county and it was nearby, actually.

We let Drew know there was potentially another local option, but cautioned him that we might not have any control whether he could attend. Drew actually had a friend at the alternative high school. He talked to his friend and did some homework online. His conclusion was that it would be good for him.

The principal at Drew's high school had been wonderfully supportive of our situation from the beginning, when Drew first needed homebound instruction in ninth, and again in tenth grade. We met with him and the Director of Secondary Instruction before the school year began to discuss our options. They saw the new "Drew" for the first time and were quite impressed with his transition. Their first choice was for Drew to stay at the public high school. Academically, it would have been much better. I'm not sure if they got many requests from parents and students to be sent to the alternative high school. Students were sent there when they were not successful in the larger high school setting. There were various reasons for this, but many were for behavioral issues or academic struggles. Drew had neither of these troubles.

Our research and later, our experience, would show that this was an excellent school for kids who had trouble fitting in at their public schools. We finally did convince the principal that the alternative high school would be a good fit for Drew. I don't think it was a sure thing administratively or easy budget-wise, but the principal made it happen.

Changing schools was an incredible growth experience for Drew. He was no longer plagued by the intense anxiety he felt every moment in school. When he did experience anxiety, the alternative high school was set up to accommodate this, and he could go to a different classroom until he felt better. Only one student at the new school knew Drew was trans, and she happened to be a good friend from middle school. She kept his secret. Bathrooms were not an issue—he used the boys—nobody cared or had reason to think he should use anything but the boy's room. Physical education was modified specifically for this school so that kids didn't have to change clothes—another problem solved.

Drew made friends and reengaged in class. He was asking questions again and voicing opinions. It was a really good year. The alternative high school exceeded our expectations. Only staff that needed to know were told Drew's situation. One member of the staff knew Drew from before his transition. There weren't any problems, only goodness. He even got a job at a grocery store and earned A's in school while holding down a part-time job.

As we watched Drew get on the school bus the last day of school, we were overwhelmed. He did it! He made it through the entire year! This was the first time since seventh grade that Drew was able to complete the school year without requiring homebound instruction.

We all assumed Drew would return in twelfth grade to finish high school, but he surprised us during the summer when he said he wanted to go back to the public high school. He wanted to prepare for college and the alternative high school wasn't really college prep. Drew could obtain his high school diploma there, but he wanted more. He wanted the possibility of getting into a good college. We were a little trepid about changing the plan. Developmentally, the alternative high school seemed to be the safest place, and he had such a good year.

Drew insisted that he wanted the option to switch. So, we met with the staff at his former high school. Again, the principal was very supportive. He, too, had assumed Drew was going back to the alternative school and had it all lined up. The principal went the extra mile. He saw Drew's determination and desire to attend college and made an offer I think Drew couldn't refuse. The principal offered to hold Drew's seat at the alternative school while Drew tried returning to the high school. The offer solidified Drew's decision to come back.

There could have been issues with bathrooms, locker rooms, and disclosing Drew's situation to staff, but the principal was not one to make an issue where there wasn't one. It helped everyone that we had all our ducks in a row, including Drew's corrected birth certificate, which identified him as a male.

The principal had one caveat, which Drew took seriously; let the principal know of any problems early on so that something could be done about them. We knew all too well that Drew had made assumptions that staff knew about problems such as bullying when they actually did not. I think the successful experience in eleventh grade recharged Drew's self-esteem enough to be proactive and constructive.

Returning to his old school was difficult, but he wanted to improve his chances of getting into a good college. It was socially and emotionally challenging. The principal was open to conducting training for all the staff and students, but Drew didn't want that. He wanted to get through his senior year quietly, without drawing any attention to himself. He had no friends at school and he lived in constant fear that the bullying and teasing he experienced in the past would return. Thankfully, it didn't. In fact, the principal brought to our attention an incident that occurred early in the school year, which made us aware that the students know Drew is the same person who attended the high school in ninth and tenth grade as a girl. In the months that followed, there were no problems or bullying. I credit the principal, staff, and the rest of the administration for doing their jobs really well and looking out for all of their students.

Drew thrived academically in twelfth grade. He occasionally had trouble with anxiety, but for the most part enjoyed his classes and the challenge. For several years, when he struggled with the symptoms of ADD and the overwhelm of coming to terms with being transgender, he began to think he wasn't very smart and said so. He *is* smart and was named to the high honor roll. He has been accepted at his choice of colleges, including the most competitive program at a prestigious university, and has won scholarships.

Behind the scenes over the years, we've worked with Drew's guidance counselor who has looked out for Drew and has done a fabulous job guiding him through this period. I know she has made a difference because Drew went to her without prompting.

The whole staff—from the attendance desk to the nurse to the teachers that taught Drew both at school and when he was home-bound to the administrators—is to be commended for keeping it simple, positive, and safe. Drew came home on the first day and said he saw a sticker from the Q Center in a classroom—an LGBT Safe Space sticker. The school got it right.

As a volunteer at the Q Center and co-facilitator of the Trans-Parent group, I have seen many schools that are still not supportive and are still not getting it right. I have seen kids drop out of school because going to school is so difficult when the administration refuses to accept them and affirm their gender identity. I want to shout my praises from the rooftop about how accepting and accommodating Drew's school has been, but I can't. Not yet. Drew wanted to get through high school without drawing any attention to himself, so we have expressed our appreciation quietly. It is wonderful that they took such good care of our Drew, not for the public recognition or praise, but because they are simply good people and educators who care about kids—and know it is the right thing to do.

Today, Drew is not only looking forward to college in the fall, he is also looking forward to living out the rest of his life. What he writes in a scholarship essay speaks volumes:

> *Though I've dealt with challenges, I've found support*
> *everywhere I turned. My family, friends, school, and the*

*Q Center have helped me through everything that's been thrown my way. Not everyone has received the opportunities and encouragement that I have and I want to help them in any way I can. Whether it be going out of my way to help others or just cheering someone up when they're down, I want to make other people's lives better. I want to pay forward all that I have received in my life to everyone else.*

*The first step towards helping people is practicing basic kindness and respect. Remember the things you have been taught as a child. If you can't say something nice, don't say anything at all. Treat others the way you want to be treated. Don't make assumptions. These are all simple concepts but they seem to be fading out of practice. Treating others right can start a chain reaction. When treated with kindness and respect, a person can think to themselves, "wow, that made me feel good. I need to start treating others like that." They then pass on that kindness to someone else who then passes it on to someone else and so on. Unfortunately these things aren't as common practice as they should be, but the only way to change that is to start by changing ourselves.*

*Another key to paying it forward is taking an active role in helping people. That means not just standing by and hoping others will change things for you. You have to take action. You have to take real steps to help, whether that is through activism or just volunteering to help at your local soup kitchen. It doesn't matter if it's big or small, anything helps. You don't have to devote your life to it, just do something. Every little bit adds up and can really make a difference in the world. Don't doubt yourself; you can make a change.*

*Last of all; don't wait for it to get bad to do good. Take notice of what's going on around you. Things might be okay, but they could always be better. If you do not maintain the good that you do it will not last. Some things require continuous effort. Many problems such as hunger, poverty, and abuse are on an ongoing downward spiral. You can't fix them all at once. If not taken care of, they will just continue to get worse. A certain situation could be okay right now but that doesn't mean it will be fine a week from now or even a year from now.*

*It is very important to me to pay forward all that I have received. I have been very lucky in my life but many people have not. I want to do my part to help those around me and help make for a better tomorrow. I will try and do what I can to make other people's lives better.*

We could not be more proud of our son.

# Chapter 13

# What about Work?

*Trust each other again and again. When the trust level gets high enough, people transcend apparent limits, discovering new and awesome abilities for which they were previously unaware.*

—David Armistead

Two years ago, in 2011, Vince and I were seated together at a company award banquet, both present to receive a very significant honor. Special Recognition Awards are given to a handful of employees each year for substantial contributions to the company. A formal ceremony follows lunch, when the vice president invites each award recipient to the podium. A summary of the employee's contributions or accomplishments are read, the award is presented, and photos are taken. My award was for a project I led to process more than nine-hundred software license requests for key business programs. Vince was being recognized for saving his program almost a half million dollars.

We looked at each other across the table and smiled a knowing smile. The accomplishments we were being recognized for at work were nothing compared to what we had accomplished at home.

We received these awards during one of the most difficult periods of our journey.

It is a wonder we survived it all and didn't lose our minds. It is an even greater wonder that we didn't lose our jobs.

While we could have become under-performing employees coasting during a time of personal crisis, Lockheed Martin provided a flexible environment, which allowed us to do more than get by. We were able to do our jobs at a level deserving of awards! This says as much about Lockheed Martin as it does about us. Accommodations like flextime, a part-time schedule and telecommuting, in addition to Lockheed Martin's commitment to diversity and inclusion, made it possible.

We feel this part of the story is important for people to hear who are both employers and employees. We hold up Lockheed Martin as a model place to work. The people, policies, and environment not only made our lives bearable, but allowed us to thrive as good employees despite the personal challenges we faced during Drew's transition (and before that during Billy's troubled teen years.)

Any personal or family crisis, not just supporting a transgender child, can impact a person's ability to go to work every day.

There is a lot an employer can do to create an environment where employees can bring their whole selves to work. If it could be done, our experience was that Lockheed Martin did it. We'd like to share some of what Lockheed Martin did, which allowed us to keep our jobs and our sanity. Some were big things, some were small. Collectively, they worked.

## Finding Help: We Weren't Alone

Our balancing act at work began in 2005 with our oldest son, Billy. Our crisis was one that all too many of us can relate to. Billy became defiant and started using drugs. We sought counseling for him and for ourselves. We didn't know where to begin, so, we simply started with the Employee Assistance Program (EAP) at work.

I credit the EAP with pointing us ultimately to the 12-step program for parents called Families Anonymous mentioned earlier in this book. FA continues to this day to provide us with the skills, support, and faith we need to live our lives successfully. The EAP program also started us down the road with counseling for Billy.

The EAP provided anonymity. We could share the difficulties that our family was facing and be assured that our employer and colleagues would not know. We were directed to resources, therapists, and programs, and nobody else had to know about it.

Eventually, however, Vince and I had to rely on our managers; we had to share what was going on in our lives. The nature of what we were dealing with was unpredictable, and, at times, life-or-death. To manage it all, we needed to flex our schedules around appointments and spend more time at home. As in most business environments, we couldn't just come and go, and disappear for hours, without saying something. Our managers made it easy for us to leave without consequence and always with dignity. They didn't disappoint. They were supportive and understanding, telling us that our family comes first. They worked with us to determine what kind of accommodations would be necessary to get our jobs done while still meeting our family's needs.

We both dropped down to a part time schedule—thirty hours per week instead of forty. The nature of what we were dealing with at home was so unpredictable; we often had to miss an entire day or at least part of a day. When things were running smoothly at home, we could work more than thirty hours and get paid for it; however, if it was a particularly challenging week, we only had to account for thirty. This flexibility was a huge relief for both of us and took the pressure off. Most of the time we managed to work more than thirty, but it was a blessing to know we didn't have to if we couldn't.

All employees have the option of a flexible work schedule and are not bound by a nine-to-five schedule Monday through Friday, unless it is necessary to serve the customer. As long as we got our jobs done, and met our schedules and commitments, it didn't matter if we worked in the middle of the night or on the weekends. The reality of our situation required working a lot of late nights and weekends.

In addition to my flexible schedule, I was also given permission to telecommute, which my job was already well-suited for. Most of my colleagues were at other locations and we generally conducted business by phone, email, or teleconference. If I called in from home it was no different than if I called in from my desk at the office.

Drew received homebound instruction for much of eighth through tenth grade. By being allowed to telecommute, I was able to be there for Drew not only for the two hours a day that he met with a tutor; I was able to be there for him all the time. In the early years, his depression was so severe, it was not in his best interest to be left alone at all. If I had to go into the office for eight hours a day, I would never have been able to concentrate. I would have been worried sick and calling constantly to check on him. Tele-commuting provided safety, security, and peace of mind. I was able to concentrate, be productive, and be home with my son while I got my job done.

In return for all of the flexibility and accommodations, Lock-heed Martin got two very dedicated and appreciative employees. We were filled with gratitude and wanted to show that their trust in us was warranted. As such, we worked longer and harder than we probably ever would have (or could have) in the office.

I remember many sleepless nights as we dealt with the chal-lenges of Drew's transition. If I couldn't sleep, I would sit at the computer and get some work done. It's not that I was a workahol-ic; this actually helped me to deal with our situation. I would often lie in bed mulling over a situation, worrying about what was going to happen, wondering how we would deal with it. I just couldn't turn my mind off. By getting out of bed and solving a work prob-lem, I was able to take my mind off the personal problem, accom-plish something I could feel good about, and eventually get tired enough to sleep. Win-win for both me and my employer.

I set up my home office in a corner of the kitchen so that my Lockheed Martin computer was always nearby. I kept the sound turned up and could hear whenever an email or instant message came in. If something came through, I would respond to it no matter what time it was. If I was available, it would get done. I had the freedom and flexibility to work around my family's needs. In return, I used that flexibility to get the job done when it was needed. The person working late who would send me an email at 8 or 9 p.m. probably wouldn't expect an answer until the morning—but they would get one minutes later and work would continue to get done.

Vince's manager, administrative assistant, and colleagues were every bit as accommodating and supportive as mine. Although the nature of his job didn't allow for telecommuting, the part-time and flexible schedule allowed him to put our family situation first and still give one hundred percent at work.

We hope our personal experience is an inspiration for Lockheed Martin and other companies reading this to continue doing the right thing. This makes a strong business case for other employers about how a flexible, inclusive work environment allows employees to feel genuinely valued and able to perform at their best … contributing to the bottom line. For Lockheed Martin, this account provides validation that its policies are effective and produce the intended results.

At the time, it was most important to me to be the fully present mom my son needed. Because Lockheed Martin supported me in this regard, I was, in return, able to be the employee they needed.

## Allies at the Office

An important part of our story is how we were supported by our employer and surrounded by allies at work before we became active allies ourselves.

Dealing with the challenges of having a transgender child was very lonely for a while. For reasons already shared, we were never sure who was a safe person to talk to. The reality of our situation required us to flex our schedules and be out for hours or days at a time. Although we had the accommodations in place to allow this, we worked in a team environment and had many friends in the office. It was awkward to constantly leave or flex without offering any explanation, at least to some colleagues. It also wasn't our nature. We worked well as a team because of our relationships and communication. To maintain this, Vince and I eventually had to risk opening up and share what was going on.

We began to feel more and more comfortable letting people know, not trying to burden anyone with the really intense stuff. We found at work what we had found elsewhere: compassion, acceptance, and occasionally somebody with a similar experience. Many colleagues were curious and asked questions. Some appeared uncomfortable and did not.

We found compassion at work when we were probably the most vulnerable we have ever been in our lives. Something I've learned over and over again: feel the fear and do it anyway. Push through the discomfort. Have the conversation. People usually surprise me, more in a good way than bad.

Coming clean allowed us to breathe. We no longer had to keep our secret.


## It Gets Better: by giving back, we got more in return

As things became better for us, Vince and I were able to start giving back. We both got involved in Lockheed Martin's local PRIDE organization. I became very involved. I was named the local site ambassador for PRIDE and the community outreach coordinator for our business area. I represented the company at several national events and worked on developing and implementing safe space programs and other initiatives.

Lockheed Martin invited me to attend the LGBT Leadership Forum held at corporate headquarters. There, I saw firsthand that Lockheed Martin's commitment to diversity and inclusion was a genuine belief of the leadership; not driven by a government mandate or because it is the politically correct thing to do. One by one, our executive leaders spoke and shared personal stories of their family members', or their own, ties to the LGBT community. Stories were shared that reinforced their personal commitment to fostering a work environment that respects and values all employees. I was proud to be part of this and excited about the plans we made for the upcoming year.

At the LGBT Leadership Forum, I was also asked to participate in filming the company's *It Gets Better* video. As you've read, our son's story is truly an example of how it does get better. As I prepared for the video shoot, I wrote a two-page summary of our story. I've been asked on numerous occasions to share that story in both small and large groups. It is remarkable how sharing our story gets others to open up. What is even more remarkable is how many people have come forward with similar stories. I thought I was the only person who knew or loved a transgender person—especially at my workplace. I discovered how wrong I was! Turns out many of my colleagues are transgender or have a child, sibling, or close friend who is transgender. Many also kept this secret. They too thought they were the only one and didn't know what the response would be if they shared.

Some people may wonder, "Well, why do you need to share? Why does it matter?" It shouldn't, but it does. In a study measuring corporate culture, it was determined that regular "water cooler" conversations cover social life (89 percent), spouses (80 percent), and children (78 percent.) Think about the last time you went to a meeting or gathered around the coffee at the office. Before the meeting starts or while you were waiting to pour your beverage, the conversation likely centered on your social life, spouse, or children. What if you felt you could not participate in these conversations because you, your spouse, or your child is LGBT? You may be unsure whether your colleagues have a negative bias that could impact your career or relationship. I lived in fear for a long time thinking that my son would be judged or rejected for being trans, or I would be judged or rejected for supporting and loving him. So I did not engage, I kept quiet rather than take the risk.

At a workplace, especially when working in team environments, you'll never get the best from an employee if they cannot fully express themselves and feel safe being who they are.

## Safe Spaces

You usually can't just look at somebody and know whether or not they are accepting. You can't go into a room and automatically know it's a safe space where you can express who you are and not be judged or criticized. You can't look at somebody you haven't met and know they are an ally unless there is some outward sign telling you so. This is why many schools, colleges, workplaces, and community organizations conduct "safe space campaigns". Last year at Lockheed Martin, we conducted two safe space campaigns with lanyards and PRIDE mugs.

Safe space campaigns are one of many ways that individual employees can reinforce an inclusive environment in their work area. By having and displaying a PRIDE mug or wearing a PRIDE lanyard, you send the message that you are someone who values diversity, openness, and acceptance. It is a quiet, subtle way to let others know, "You can be who you are with me. I am open and accepting and believe we are all valued and equally important."

Lockheed Martin has cultivated a culture where it is safe to let change happen at a natural pace. Wearing a PRIDE lanyard or displaying a PRIDE mug was not company policy, nor was it an obligation. In fact, that would be counter-productive. We didn't want to hand them out or make anybody feel obligated to participate. I, for one, would want to be sure that anyone displaying a mug or wearing a lanyard chose to do so because they truly believed what they represent. These safe space campaigns are a voluntary way for allies to show their support.

I was blown away with the turn out and requests for lanyards and mugs. My site was the first to launch the mug campaign. Within the first week, I went through my entire inventory. I had more mugs shipped to me and went through the second supply within a week's time. I introduced the campaign in a presentation and I put a short paragraph in the weekly newsletter. People had to take action to actually request them, and they did! In fact, the program had to be reevaluated because there wasn't budget to support this much participation. Absolutely awesome problem!

The demand for lanyards and mugs included a diverse mix of people from the factory floor to senior management, young and old. This says to me that Lockheed Martin is succeeding in creating a culture and workplace where people can feel comfortable being who they are.

## Out for Work

Lockheed Martin asked me to represent the company at the Out for Work 2012 National Conference. Out for Work is a non-profit organization dedicated to helping LGBT students make the transition from college to the workplace. I had been to recruiting conferences before, but this one was different because I was asked to be a panelist and speak about my experience as a parent and as an ally in the workplace. This wasn't just about being an engineer and recruiting other engineers. This was about being a human being, and how my family and all that I truly value intersected with my career.

After sharing my story, dozens of LGBT college students and allies wanted to talk to me, wanted a hug, wanted to know how and why I was able to be so accepting of my son. They wanted to share their personal experiences coming out to their parents, whether those experiences were good, bad, or still being avoided.

I left the Out for Work Conference feeling proud of Lockheed Martin and certain that Vince and I were making a difference; that telling our story is important. I felt like I had briefly been a mom to three hundred eighty college students, many of whom needed to hear and know they are OK. That struck me so deeply, because these young people are better than OK; they are amazing and perfect as they are.

I remember being on stage and looking around the room full of beautiful, brilliant faces. All of them could be my son. All of them could be any one of our sons or daughters. This room full of young people perfectly represented the diversity of all our children; each with their different stories, their unique experiences, cultures, and families. Yet they also shared a common bond that brought them together at this conference.

These were amazing, beautiful, smart, perfect, incredible souls. Their resumes rivaled any that I had seen before, yet it was their hearts shining through that I'll never forget. As we spoke one-on-one throughout the remainder of the conference, many shared their private stories of hiding from their friends and family or being rejected. Others had positive stories to tell, but deeply appreciated my story and my son's because they had seen the pain in others.

We have many reasons for choosing to share our story, but the Out for Work Conference sparked something inside me, which took us from talking about writing a book to actually doing it. The experience ultimately led me to leave the security of my career and follow a deeper calling.

## Human Rights Campaign 2012 National Dinner

The morning I returned to work after the Out for Work Conference, I found the following email in my inbox:

> *Hi Terri,*
>
> *I hope all is well with you! We received an urgent request from our Corporate Diversity/Inclusion office to help them identify an Electronic Systems representative to attend the upcoming HRC dinner this Saturday, October 6th in Washington DC.*
>
> *We wanted to see if you would be interested in attending -- although we know this would mean travel for you and it's on a weekend!*

I couldn't believe my good fortune! It took me no time to send off my response:

> *Good morning. YES, YES, YES!!! Forgive my enthusiasm, but I just returned from Out for Work and I cannot begin to express the impact it had on me. While at OFW I had the privilege of meeting and speaking at length with Joe*

*Solmonese (former president of HRC.) For many reasons, on so many levels, I would be proud and excited to represent ES at the HRC dinner.*

    *Please let me know what I need to do to help make the arrangements. Thank you!*

Vince was invited to join me as my guest. He was just as excited. Part of the excitement was due to this being our first ever black-tie event. The last time Vince put on a tux was during the series of weddings that followed ours back in the late eighties and early nineties! The excitement and enormity of this event turned out to be far more than just an opportunity to dress up.

The Human Rights Campaign, HRC, is the largest civil rights organization working to achieve equality for LGBT Americans. HRC boasts more than one and a half million members and supporters nationwide. Founded in 1980, HRC advocates on behalf of LGBT Americans, mobilizes grassroots actions in diverse communities, invests strategically to elect fair-minded individuals to office, and educates the public about LGBT issues.

The dinner speakers were passionate and inspiring. I encourage you to watch every one of these speeches on YouTube; they are really worth your time. Corey Booker, the mayor of Newark, N.J., delivered a powerful keynote speech. Sally Field received the *Ally for Equality Award*. Sam Greisman, Sally Field's son, introduced Sally; his story and introduction were wonderful! Ben Jealous received the *National Equality Award* on behalf of the NAACP. Oscar-winning screenwriter Dustin Lance Black shared a moving personal story of his coming out experience, of the loss of his gay older brother, and the importance of sharing our personal stories. Chad Griffin, president of HRC, gave a powerful speech about the work Human Rights Campaign is doing. So inspiring—every one of them!

Several other celebrities, activists, and supporters of the movement toward equality also spoke at the event.

There was a performance by Cirque du Soleil, which was incredible. I was so blown away by what they were able to do on the HRC dinner stage that I absolutely have to get to one of their shows some day!

I figured the dinner was a fundraising event, but didn't realize the scope of the benefit until that night. In addition to a silent auction, live auction, and Lexus raffle, there was a drive that lasted maybe fifteen or twenty minutes that raised nearly four-hundred thousand dollars from attendees. The proceeds from that individual drive went toward a campaign in the four states where marriage equality was on the ballot: Maine, Minnesota, Maryland, and Washington. Clearly the donations were put to good use as marriage equality passed in all four states!

Our experience at the HRC National Dinner was eye-opening and inspiring. Everything about it was spectacular. I hope there are many more such events in my future. Our appreciation of HRC and commitment to their efforts was solidified when we became members of the HRC Federal Club that night.

It was long before that evening; however, that HRC had a direct impact on our lives and the lives of others. I credit HRC and its Corporate Equality Index (CEI) with motivating Lockheed Martin and hundreds of other employers to add transgender-inclusive policies and protections, including insurance coverage.

HRC's CEI is the national benchmarking tool on corporate policies and practices related to LGBT employees. The CEI index ranks employers, from zero to one hundred. Specific criteria are used in the calculation, measuring policies, benefits, and company practices. Companies strive for a perfect score of one hundred.

The CEI has propelled equality forward by sparking competition and raising awareness about what inequalities persist. In 2012, HRC raised the bar and toughened its criteria, requiring employers to offer transgender inclusive benefits in order to earn or maintain a perfect score of one hundred.

In 2012, Lockheed Martin added transgender benefits and coverage for gender reassignment surgery. I can only assume LM did not want to lose its perfect score on the CEI. Our experience with Lockheed Martin over the years leads us to believe the company would have added these benefits eventually. We salute HRC for simply speeding up the process.

Although the experiences written about in this book ultimately led to us leaving the security of our careers with Lockheed Martin, Vince and I will be forever grateful for the support and opportunities this corporation provided.

**Chapter 14**

# Concluding Thoughts

*As spiritual beings having a human experience; compassion
and acceptance of the endless and often misunderstood
variations and complexities of humans is necessary.*
—*Vince Cook*

The famous life coach, Martha Beck, first explained to me (in her book *Steering by Starlight*) how a butterfly needs to struggle when it emerges from its chrysalis. Since then, I have learned that the struggle actually inflates, or forces fluid, into the butterfly's wings allowing them to expand to their mature size and shape. Without the struggle, the butterfly's wings remain small and incapable of flight. Without the ability to fly, the butterfly's life is limited to its ability to walk the earth and find food, missing the potential an aerial life promises.

If I think of accepting my transgender son as my chrysalis, I can better appreciate all that my family has been through and see it for what it is—a gift. Like the butterfly, I faced three outcomes: to never emerge, to make it out incapable of flight, or to gloriously succeed and experience the beauty of a full life.

For me, to never emerge from my chrysalis would have been to succumb to my fears and limiting beliefs. I would have suffered in silence—afraid of judgment, ridicule, and whatever nastiness my mind could invent. I would die inside my chrysalis.

Then there would be the easy way out. That is, to side with the majority of people who know very little about being transgender. That would be easy because it would have coincided with my ignorance and limiting beliefs. I wanted to reject the notion that the child I raised for fifteen years could actually be my son and not my daughter. I would survive, but my family would suffer. I don't know if my son would have survived. Like the little boy who cuts the chrysalis to help the butterfly, he doesn't know what he's doing—the butterfly suffers its whole life. Taking the easy way out might have ruined my relationship with my son and my whole family.

Our actual struggle, which Terri and I document in this book, has formed and strengthened my wings so that I can fly. I clearly know now that suppressing and rejecting transgender children robs them of their childhood and adds tremendously to the burden of transition later in life. My pain, my struggle has been to shed my limiting beliefs through education and reaching out, to experience the loss of a daughter and the gaining of a son, to develop a heartfelt compassion for the challenges of being transgender, and to openly accept the same risk of rejection and opposition my son faces in an imperfect world.

I truly believe my family is more loving and closer than it would have been had we not had this challenge. But, there is another message.

Before Drew, Terri and I faced a more common parenting crisis with our older son, Billy. Handling drug abuse and reckless behavior for me as a parent was in many ways similar to the situation with Drew. Certainly, there is a lot of judgment and ignorance related to those issues. I could have shut down and consumed myself with anger, resentment, and shame. I could have taken an easy route that sought to avoid criticism, but destroyed my relationship with Billy and possibly the family. Or I could have done what I eventually did, which was struggle as I should struggle—to shed my limiting beliefs through education and reaching out, to develop personal boundaries while staying engaged, to allow my son to experience the consequences of his choices, and to develop a heartfelt compassion for the difficulty of his recovery. We love the man who symbolically emerged from his own chrysalis better, wiser, and more loving. In his recovery, Billy gave us a beautiful song, *How to Live*. We've included the lyrics at the end of this chapter for you to enjoy. Although Billy wrote the song to reflect the lessons he learned in his recovery, the song has become symbolic of how we have all learned how to live. The lyrics apply not only to Billy, but also to Drew, Terri and me.

My experience with Billy gave me the critical parenting skills and thick skin to support Drew's needs more effectively—my strong wings.

The lesson of the chrysalis applies to Drew and other children in similar situations, but from a different perspective. The anxiety of not knowing the process, the means of achieving your transition into acceptance can be overwhelming. Before Drew even knew there was a transition to come, he felt it was hopeless and wanted to end it all. For Drew, the challenge was being transgender; for other kids, the challenges could be their sexual orientation, race, religion, weight, or something else. Our young people need to know that when they struggle in order to find peace, understanding, and acceptance, it will be a process that can eventually lead them to reach their greatest potential.

It's not true that helping the butterfly always hurts the butterfly. The chrysalis can prove to be too tough for the butterfly to break through. At the right moment, when the butterfly has put in enough effort, help is appropriate and can actually save the butterfly or make it easier.

Allies and angels have served this helpful role in my struggle to support Drew and his brother. For a real chrysalis, factors like a dry summer can make the chrysalis too tough for any butterfly to emerge. Likewise, elements outside of our control can make our struggles futile. Allies use their experience and judgment to help at the right time. Often, the right time is after we have struggled enough on our own to realize we need help.

---

### Why did we write this book?

Drew had a family that supported him and yet he almost lost his life. Vince and I can only imagine how difficult life is for many other children (and adults) who do not have their parent's support. Well actually, I don't have to imagine because I have seen it at the Q Center and elsewhere over the past few years. It's heartbreaking.

Vince and I chose to forego amniocentesis when I was pregnant with Drew because we loved, wanted, and would accept him for who he was. Fifteen years later, we renewed our acceptance of who he is. We were no stranger to tough love and setting boundaries, but if we learned anything as parents it is that all children are unique. We didn't know what the right approach was for Drew, but we had learned to listen to him, to keep an open mind, to do our homework, to reach out for help, and to not be timid when it came time to act.

I have come to understand that most people have no idea what it means to be transgender. I also discovered that most people have no idea of the challenges faced by transgender individuals. By not knowing, you are (perhaps unconsciously) contributing to the problem and the pain of others.

I believe the words of Maya Angelou, "*When you know better, you do better.*" I hope that our story, and all our efforts to publicize it, will help people to know better. I do believe in humanity and I have no doubt that people will do better when they know better—regarding transgender people and all other marginalized populations.

Many people *think* they know what it means to be transgender, but my experience has been that many who think they know are completely misinformed. As a result, their misunderstanding perpetuates myths, fears, and stereotypes, which cause tremendous harm to others. Many people who *think* they know what it means to be transgender believe it is a choice. They think a transgender person is one who was born a girl and decides she would rather be a boy, so she chooses to have a sex change from female-to-male. Or conversely, they think it is someone born a boy who decides he would rather be a girl, so he chooses to have a sex change from male-to-female.

What many fail to understand is that gender identity is permanently developed in the brain and not directly related to your sex organs. Being transgender is a medical condition that nobody would choose to have. When what is between your ears, your brain's physical development, does not match what is between your legs, it causes tremendous pain, anxiety, and dysphoria. And what is worse, unlike with other medical conditions, there is little sympathy, compassion, support, or understanding from society. Often, family members and uninformed medical professionals reject transgender people as well.

The choice—the decision—for transgender people is to choose to understand and accept the medical condition they were born with; to choose to work with trained professionals to follow the standards of care, which lead to a diagnosis and appropriate treatment; to choose to endure the ridicule from much of society; and to choose to live and make the best of a medical condition that no one would choose to have. The appropriate treatments vary depending on the individual. Unfortunately, the appropriate treatments are often not accessible, or are accessible but denied, to many people.

Imagine being born with a medical condition that you could not control and you did nothing to cause. Many transgender people experience so much pain and difficulty that forty-one percent attempt suicide. Imagine that rather than receiving empathy, support, and compassion for your medical condition, you received rejection, harassment, discrimination, and acts of violence against you. To top it off, imagine that there were no laws to protect you from this injustice. In thirty-three states, including our home state of New York, it is actually legal to be fired, denied housing or services, and discriminated against if you are transgender.

Sadly, because they are transgender, people are often treated harshly and denied the dignity and equality that every person deserves.

I've learned a lot over the past few years because I had to learn—because my child's life depended on it. My son's struggle to understand, accept, and simply be who he is, almost cost him his life. Our ability as parents to understand, accept, and help him has played a part in saving his life.

The overarching message is that transgender awareness saves lives. I hope by reading our story you have come to understand something you may not otherwise have been exposed to nor had a need to learn. By understanding and accepting, you have the potential to save *MANY* lives—even if you don't personally have a transgender friend or loved one.

For change, true equality, and an end to discrimination, we need to normalize being transgender so that it is just another celebrated element of diversity. Our hope is that this book is read by *all* people, not just by families and friends of transgender individuals.

When you've finished reading this book, we hope you'll be an ally and pass it along to a friend. Give them the opportunity to learn something they might not otherwise have been exposed to or had a need to learn. Give them the chance to know better and do better.

### Sharing our story and being a bridge

Another reason Vince and I shared our story is because we believe we can be a bridge. Even after reading our story, you may not fully understand being transgender or having a loved one who is transgender, but you can possibly relate to us as parents or as people. We hope, as you read our story, you could relate to us and see that we are good parents doing the best we can. We are a loving couple who have worked hard throughout our lives and have been kind and giving in our relationships with family, friends, neighbors, and coworkers. We love our children deeply and unconditionally. If you can see a bit of yourself in us, then perhaps you can accept our child. Drew deserves the same privileges, freedoms, rights, and opportunities as all other children. We hope that by getting to know us we've affirmed your belief that *all* people are beautiful, valued, worthwhile human beings deserving of love, of dignity, and of protection from discrimination.

It is through personal and professional relationships—through getting to know actual transgender people and their loved ones—that we can break down the myths, lies, fears, and stereotypes that lead to discrimination. That's why we've taken this risk to expose ourselves and our vulnerabilities; to let you get to know us.

Anybody can unlearn limiting beliefs and previously held misconceptions.

Stories can provide an understanding of the inner workings of different types of people. The number of people willing to share their stories is growing. Although every story is unique, each adds to the body of knowledge.

We were victims of a lack of awareness. We've talked about the surprise we felt when our son came to us and said he was transgender. Vince and I wish we had been better prepared. Our family and the experts we called upon struggled for almost two years after Drew's suicide attempt to understand what was wrong.

Our story will hopefully help other parents and families with a loved one who is transgender by letting them know they are not alone, helping them learn from our experience, and giving them hope that they too can be happy.

But reaching transgender people and their families with our story is just the beginning. As a bridge, we hope to reach an even wider audience. Many of the fears and difficulties of being transgender are compounded by the lack of awareness and acceptance in our society. A more general public understanding and acceptance will make it easier for transgender people and their families to find help and live a full life.

**How were we changed? Ending the Judgment**

Because I now know what it feels like to be judged, misunderstood, rejected, and marginalized as Drew's mom, I've come to feel more compassion toward and connectedness to others. Vince and I became people we previously didn't understand—the parents of a transgender youth. We became marginalized when previously we were accepted, liked, and in the privileged group. I now know what it feels like to be on both sides.

Our life lessons from having a transgender son apply far beyond the transgender and LGBT community.

I recognized how often we judge people that we don't know and don't really know anything about—judgments based on meanings we apply to somebody's appearance, circumstances, or situation. If somebody is covered with piercings or tattoos, does that bring up a judgment? What about if somebody is an addict or has a child who is an addict? How about a stay-at-home mom or a mom who chooses to work outside the home and send her child to daycare? What about a homeless person? An unemployed person? An overweight person? A gay person? Really there are so many things, big and small, that can result in judgment or fear or feeling uncomfortable around somebody.

Abraham Lincoln has been quoted as saying, "*I don't like that man. I must get to know him better.*"

I think about my beautiful boy and how somebody might judge him when they don't know him. I think of how I hope they will open their hearts and minds and get to know the person inside, not stop at the circumstance that they don't understand (being transgender.) With this perspective, I now see all people differently and it causes me to put away my judgments and assume nothing until I get to know the person.

I now challenge myths and know everything is not black or white, right or wrong. I assume nothing is binary and try to catch myself whenever I fall into the trap of measuring against society's norms. I'm not perfect and I'm not a saint, but I want to be the kind of person that I hope my children encounter throughout their lives.

### About Fear

We talked a lot about how we suffer in silence when we fail to reach out for help. Our experiences taught us the importance of reaching out. There will undoubtedly be people who accuse us of being bad parents or criticize us for something they feel we did wrong, but by not reaching out, by not risking criticism or rejection to find help, we might never have found the truth about being transgender, or happiness as a family.

What we learned at support groups—Families Anonymous, PFLAG, and the Q Center's TransParent group—was that we're not alone. Other people in our community were going through similar problems. People were in different phases and each gave us confidence and hope because we could see where we stood in our experience. We all need help.

The scientific knowledge base of transgender issues is rapidly evolving, but we have to make decisions now about how to best love and support our children. We can't wait for the world to catch up, there is too much at stake in our children's lives.

We lost so much time to fear, and suffered so much because of fear. In the end, much of our fear was of imagined events, reactions, or outcomes that did not happen. Most of our actual experiences have been positive or at least neutral. Still, the fear is there.

In *Steering by Starlight*, Martha Beck talks about the personal importance of dissolving lies when she commands, *"Question every thought that causes suffering and test it against your own sense of truth."*

How many times did I avoid running into old friends and neighbors in the grocery store, or tiptoe around conversations with new friends to avoid disclosing that my son is transgender? There may be nothing real to fear in those particular situations—the person I am avoiding or speaking to may not discriminate against me or expose my son to harm by disclosing his identity. However, my fear of exposing myself in what may actually be a safe place is carried over from past real experiences (my own and others') of physical violence, rejection, or discrimination.

It is imperative to point out that there are stark reasons to fear. Violence, harassment, discrimination, and rejection of transpeople are very real. The statistics of murder and violence and hate crimes against the transgender community are horrifying. I don't want to minimize this dangerous reality or disrespect the cruelty others have faced by bringing attention to my family's positive encounters and suggesting that all fears are imagined.

Fear consumes my son. Drew just wanted to get through his senior year of high school without bringing any attention to himself. He went quietly from class to class, walking the halls alone without any friends. In reality, the friends he might have made if he risked talking with someone may have become good friends; they might have been kind and accepting. However, after years of being bullied, tormented, pushed around, and told repeatedly that he's a loser and a freak, he chose to get through his senior year quietly, sitting and walking alone rather than taking a chance and being seen. Returning to the days of bullying and rejection was an unbearable risk, and so his fear, even if imagined, won.

The way to end both the real and perceived fears is to bring them out into the open. If we spread awareness of the injustices and violent acts that are real, people will rise up to end them and create laws for equal protection. Similarly, if we express our fears of rejection and judgment, then allies will rise up to show compassion and acceptance.

And so we've shared our fears, hoping it will be a step toward ending *both* the real and imagined things we fear. It is frightening and uncomfortable to be so vulnerable, but we, as parents, are getting comfortable with being uncomfortable. Transgender people and other marginalized groups have been unjustly uncomfortable for far too long.

## Allies

Throughout our story, we refer to the allies and angels who guided us, supported us, and helped us through what was once an unthinkable journey.

What does it mean to be an ally?

Generally speaking, an ally is a member of a privileged group who takes a stand against oppression; for example: a white person who speaks out against racism or a straight person who works to end heterosexism and homophobia. An ally works to become part of social change rather than part of oppression.

We can *all* be allies. Actions big and small in our everyday lives can change people's lives and turn difficult or frightening experiences into positive ones. You don't have to be a sign-carrying, chanting, lobbying activist to be an ally. Similarly, you do not have to be in a position of power or influence. Our allies were not just people in the medical profession or schools or courts or LGBT community who helped us save our son's life. They were friends and family and business colleagues who showed compassion. They were store clerks and waiters and strangers on the street who were courteous and kind and flashed an accepting smile.

My hope is that everybody who reads this book becomes an ally. My greatest wish is that something you've read will move you to understand what it means to be an ally and take actions in your life to increase awareness, challenge oppressive attitudes and behaviors, and help others move beyond tolerance toward understanding, appreciation, and celebration of our differences.

And not just an ally to the LGBT community but an ally to all people. If you've peaked ahead to the mission statement for the Ally Project, or visited our Ally Project website (theallyproject. com) you may have noticed that the mission statement doesn't mention or restrict being an ally only within the LGBT community.

Granted, Vince and I became passionate allies after learning our son is transgender. We were blessed to find countless allies in the LGBT community who guided and supported us through what was, at times, a very difficult and painful journey. Through our experiences, we also learned firsthand of the inequities, injustices, and discrimination that still exist in the LGBT community. All of this led to our decision and commitment to help raise awareness and bring about positive change… and we became passionate allies.

It is convenient to become allies to those communities most near and dear, but all too often we, including myself, are guilty of limiting our minds and our good intentions to only those communities.

Finding love and compassion for all is a higher calling for allies, and so our definition of an ally is purposely much broader and does not unduly restrict application to only the LGBT community. If we can look beyond our differences and consider how we treat *all* people—with compassion and an open mind regardless of how we or they identify—we have hope for a world where nobody is marginalized or oppressed.

We are grateful to the allies who made a difference in our lives. Many you've read about in this book; others are listed in the Acknowledgments.

## Final Thought

At one time, this journey would have been unthinkable. Now, we are grateful and can see the hidden gifts of our experience. We have gained so much from a situation and life events that we never would have chosen for our family.

From our experience as Drew and Billy's parents, we learned that despite challenges and unsolved problems, we can do more than get by, we can thrive! In fact, difficult experiences actually can make our lives better, richer, and fuller while increasing our capacity to love, experience joy, and feel more compassion and connectedness to ourselves and others.

The butterfly carries a message of hope—its struggle has purpose. Like the butterfly, and like both our sons, we are stronger after the struggle, and we have been transformed.

**Learning my daughter is really my son taught me
who I am and who I want to be**

*I am* a compassionate human being. I am a person just like you. I have worth, just as you do. No matter who you are reading this, I assure you, we have more in common than differences.

*I want to be* somebody who never forgets the lessons and awareness gained from this experience ... someone who uses the rest of my precious life applying these lessons, who treats all with compassion, and who helps build a world full of allies.

# How to Live: A Song of Inspiration

*by Billy Cook*

*I'm so far away from*
*The boy I used to be*
*But that ain't me*
*Was never one to walk too tall*
*But the strength to carry on*
*Gets me through it all*

*So what I'm trying to say*
*Is I'm better off this way*
*Keep moving on*
*'Cause I've learned to*

*Pick it up, break it down*
*Try again, I'm making ground*
*Don't give up, pull it through*
*And always to myself be true*
*Good and bad are relative*
*I give it all I have to give*
*I think I've finally learned how to live*

*I may be a wreck when*
*I'm thinking all alone*
*But still I grow*
*And for every step back I take*

*I take two more in its place*
*Soon I'm gone*

*So I'm just trying to say*
*That I'm better off this way*
*Keep moving on*
*'Cause I've learned to*

*Pick it up, break it down*
*Try again, I'm making ground*
*Don't give up, pull it through*
*And always to myself be true*
*Good and bad are relative*
*I give it all I have to give*
*I think I've finally learned how to live*

Soon I'm Gone
Billy Cook

*All young people, regardless of sexual orientation or identity,*
*deserve a safe and supportive environment in which to*
*achieve their full potential.*
*—Harvey Milk*

If you've read this far into our book, then you've read a lot about a wonderful place called the Q Center. We can't possibly share our family's story without talking about "the Q." Throughout portions of our story, the Q is mentioned on nearly every page.

Vince and I believe our son is alive today because of the Q Center. Although many will argue that he's alive because he has us for parents, we know in our hearts that the Q helped us learn how to support him, and the Q provided a safe space for him while we were learning.

The Q Center was the first place Drew felt he fit in; where he could be himself and be accepted. It was in that safe, fun space where he began to understand and accept himself, and where he found the hope that his life could get better. The Q Center is where we saw Drew smile, laugh, relax, and just be a kid again—for the first time in years.

**The Q Center is a safe space for LGBTQ youth and allies**
… a place to go where you can be yourself
… a place to meet others who are asking questions
and finding answers
… a place you can be proud to support!

I am just a mom who loves my children with all my heart, and who wants to use our family's experience to help and educate others. At this time more than ever, however, I wish I were also a gifted writer because I'm grasping for words that will help readers feel the goose bumps and warmth I feel when I think back and see that first smile on Drew's face ... after years of struggling to exist. The Q Center, and all the wonderful staff, volunteers, and families we've met there, will forever be in our hearts.

We're not alone in being helped and changed. As a Q Center volunteer, I have seen the life-changing difference this organization has had on youth throughout Central New York.

### Giving Back

A portion of the proceeds from the sales of our book will be donated to the Q Center, so it can continue and perhaps even expand upon the services it provides. The Q Center will be mentioned in all of our marketing materials and we hope the publicity will result in more donations and support, not only for the Q Center, but for other centers like it.

### About the Q

The Q Center is located in Syracuse, N.Y., and serves a nine-county area.

The Q Center is a safe place for lesbian, gay, bisexual, transgender, and questioning (LGBTQ) youth, as well as their allies and parents to gather, share, hang out, have fun, and build healthy relationships with supportive adults and peers. The Q Center offers a number of educational and support groups, as well as counseling services, social events, HIV education and testing, suicide prevention, community outreach, and support for Gay-Straight Alliances and schools. Most importantly, the Q Center provides a space where you can be yourself. The Q Center equips LGBTQ youth to create a safer community with other young people who are all about equality.

In addition to serving youth, the Q Center is a wonderful resource for the community and for families of LGBT youth. Sadly, not all families are supportive of their LGBT children. All are welcome to join parent support groups hosted at the Q Center and take advantage of resources and programming. For youth who do not have supportive families, the Q Center is critical to their well-being. Transportation and food are provided to ensure accessibility for all.

The Q Center offers several support groups which meet regularly at the Syracuse facility, and offers youth groups in Auburn, Utica, and Watertown. The Q Center is one of only seven youth centers in the U.S. to house a David Bohnett Cyber Center, which offers youth state-of-the-art technology and technical support, making it the only center of its kind within a 240 mile radius, The Q Center also houses or sponsors a number of programs. The following list is just a sampling:

- **After-School Programs**: Drop in time every week includes tutoring, college counseling, the Eddie Future Greatness Scholarship, which provides 4 scholarships a year to college bound Q members, a large LGBTQ library, and the David Bohnett CyberCenter, offering state-of-the-art resources and technology.

- **Support Groups**: We offer weekly and biweekly support groups, such as LGBTQ Youth & Allies (ages 13-17), Steppin' Out (ages 18-22), TransYouth, TransParent, and Youth of Color, to name a few. We also offer mental health assessment & affirming mental health referrals to youth and families.

- **Outreach & Education**: The allies=strength in numbers program, our ally development program, teaches the community how to be better allies to all youth & our tent is available to all not-for-profits. Cultural competency trainings for youth serving agencies and organizations are available free of charge. Additionally, we offer support to our local Gay-Straight Alliances.

- **Special Events**: annual Pride Prom, Q Pride Celebration, trip to Albany, NY to lobby legislators, and several more. These events provide semi-structured socialization time, for youth to connect and realize they are not alone.

We are very proud to support the Q Center, and we are fortunate to have such a wonderful resource in our community.

**Links to learn more or to make a donation**

aidscommunityresources.com/content.cfm/services/youth-center

facebook.com/pages/The-Q-Center/129267220435675

theqcenter.tumblr.com

## Mission

The Ally Project is dedicated to finding practical ways to grow acceptance, compassion, and love while protecting the peaceful expression of personal identity, preferences, and rights.

By providing a fun, welcoming community rich with resources, support, and personal stories, The Ally Project strives to create a world where every person is valued and respected, moving beyond tolerance toward understanding, appreciation and celebration of our differences.

The Ally Project will serve as a resource for Allies while raising overall awareness of perceived and actual discrimination and inequality in our world. Here you'll find tools to bring about change in yourself and the world. We believe real change comes about when we can see each other as real people … no more or less important than ourselves.

Through sharing stories, partnerships with other organizations, and the power of social media, we advocate for cultural change and equality.

### So what is The Ally Project?

The Ally Project will formally launch in the fall of 2013, although our blog is active and we'd love you to follow us! We hope to create a fun, welcoming community rich with resources, support, and personal stories.

The idea for the Ally Project came about in 2012 when Terri and Vince still worked for Lockheed Martin. The company's 2012 PRIDE theme was "Stepping into the Future *Together*"—emphasizing the importance of the role allies play in advancing the dialogue and cultural change. Hoping to develop ally training,

Terri searched for resources to bring into the workplace. Although she found a wealth of material for college students and secondary schools, resources for the workplace and general community were limited. She also found primarily a collection of static lists… checklists and "do's and don'ts" and definitions intended to educate allies. Although that is important (and will be available on The Ally Project website) we wanted something more … to expand on personal stories (so we can get to know real people) and spotlight *Allies in Action* (so we can see why and how we can *all* be allies and make a difference.)

We have seen it in our own lives. Discrimination, rejection and marginalization of people are real. We were once popular, successful, accepted … some might even say upstanding members of society. When we became parents of a transgender child … and more shockingly, parents who supported their son's transition at the age of 15 … we experienced what it feels like to be judged, criticized, rejected and discriminated against. But we also saw the power to change that by getting to know people and sharing personal stories. This is not just our experience… it is strongly supported by decades of research: when people know someone who is gay or trans (or know someone they love is gay or trans) their acceptance of the LGBT community increases dramatically. The same is true for other marginalized groups.

We witnessed the change when people who already knew us considered, "Hey, that's the same old Terri (or Vince) that I've always known and loved. Maybe I should get to know a bit more about this transgender thing… because clearly the Cook family is not one I need to be afraid of or judge." When we meet new people and connect with them—maybe as parents, or engineers, or community members—we serve as a bridge that helps people understand and accept something they previously didn't understand or accept.

We have a lot of ideas for the Ally Project, and we invite you to visit theallyproject.com to share your thoughts and ideas. Please check out our site and sign up to follow the action!

**TheAllyProject.com**

# Free eBook Campaign

Our goal is to reach as many people as possible who are in a position to help save and change lives. For that reason, we are providing the *Allies & Angels* eBook for FREE to educators, social workers, health care workers, service providers, and LGBT youth center employees!

We were victims of a lack of awareness and wish we had been better prepared. Our family, and the experts we called upon, struggled for nearly two years after our son's suicide attempt to understand what was wrong.

Our desperate efforts to diagnose and manage his depression and anxiety included weekly therapy, numerous doctors and specialists, and many different prescription medications. Although we were supported by a highly qualified team of doctors, educators, and counselors, it took years to connect the dots and recognize that gender identity was the root of the problem.

However …

### Ignorance ≠ Intolerance!

More often, ignorance is merely a lack of awareness—when good people simply have not been exposed to information and experiences different from their own. We just didn't know it was possible for our son to have a male brain inside a female body. Many of the professionals we worked with didn't know either, or they knew but did not have enough experience to recognize the signs.

Children and their families often seek support for LGBT issues through school counselors, social workers, therapists, doctors, nurses, and youth center staff. The likelihood of a strong positive outcome increases when those professionals have experience or awareness of these issues. For that reason, we are sharing our story, and conducting this Free eBook Campaign, to increase awareness … and compassion.

Please spread the word and share our Free eBook Campaign with educators, social workers, health care workers, service providers, and LGBT youth center employees. More information and a Free eBook Request Form can be found at:

**alliesandangels.com/free-books**

CPSIA information can be obtained at www.ICGtesting.com
Printed in the USA
LVOW07*1928310813

350451LV00004B/8/P